Users' Guides to Human Factors and Ergonomics Methods

Risk Management:

How to Assess and Control Risk Related to Human Error in Products and Systems

By Edmond W. Israelski and William H. Muto

Published by the
HUMAN FACTORS and ERGONOMICS SOCIETY

Print ISBN 978-0-945289–03-6
E-book ISBN 978-0-945289–04-3

Published by the
Human Factors and Ergonomics Society
http://www.hfes.org

The Human Factors and Ergonomics Society is the world's largest scientific association for human factors and ergonomics researchers and practitioners, psychologists and other scientists, designers, engineers, and health-care professionals. Members address a diverse range of subject areas related to the design, development, testing and evaluation, and deployment of systems, products, tools, and environments that enhance human performance, safety, and effectiveness. HFES has more than 3,000 members worldwide, many affiliated with local, regional, and student chapters. The Society has 26 technical interest groups. Membership information can be found at http://www.hfes.org.

Library of Congress Cataloging-in-Publication Data

Names: Israelski, Edmond W., 1946- author. | Muto, William H, 1946- author.

Title: Risk management : how to assess and control risk related to human error in products and systems / by Edmond W. Israelski and William H. Muto.

Description: [Washington] : Human Factors and Ergonomics Society, [2022] | Series: Users' guides to human factors and ergonomics methods | Includes bibliographical references and index. | Summary: "From its early days, human factors has focused on the identification and prevention of human error. And yet, most human factors practitioners have not had to deal with the formal techniques, tools, and the language associated with risk analysis and risk management. While most references on risk management concentrate on failure of mechanical and electrical systems, this book concentrates on identifying and controlling human error in systems, intended as a user guide to the most common risk management tools that are applicable to a wide variety of products and systems. Among the many risk management tools mentioned, we discuss and illustrate with case studies two of the most used methodologies, FMEA (Failure Modes and Effects Analysis) and FTA (Fault Tree Analysis). Although our case studies focus on medical devices, the methods discussed are applicable to many products and systems, including those in industries such as transportation, nuclear power generation, aerospace, consumer products, and health care"-- Provided by publisher.

Identifiers: LCCN 2022034365 (print) | LCCN 2022034366 (ebook) | ISBN 9780945289036 (paperback) | ISBN 9780945289043 (ebook)

Subjects: LCSH: Risk management. | Structural failures. | System failures (Engineering) | Errors.

Classification: LCC HD61 .R56968 2022 (print) | LCC HD61 (ebook) | DDC 658.15/5--dc23/eng/20220722

LC record available at https://lccn.loc.gov/2022034365

LC ebook record available at https://lccn.loc.gov/2022034366

Users' Guides to Human Factors and Ergonomics Methods

Other Titles in This Series

USABILITY ASSESSMENT:
How to Measure the Usability of Products, Services, and Systems
Philip Kortum

WORKLOAD ASSESSMENT:
How to Diagnose Workload Issues and Enhance Performance
Gerald Matthews and Lauren E. Reinerman-Jones

QUESTIONNAIRE DESIGN:
How to Ask the right Questions of the Right People at the Right Time to Get the Information You Need
William F. Moroney and Joyce A. Cameron

TASK ANALYSIS:
How to Develop an Understanding of Work
Jack Stuster

SITUATION AWARENESS MEASUREMENT:
How to Measure Situation Awareness in Individuals and Teams
Mica R. Endsley

Available from
Human Factors and Ergonomics Society – hfes.org
Amazon.com

I dedicate this book to Linda, my loving wife of almost 50 years. She has been highly encouraging in this writing effort from the beginning and through all of the editing and has been very supportive of my career in human factors engineering. I also thank my daughters, Christin and Keri Anne, for their support and encouragement.

—Ed Israelski

Unending gratitude goes to my mentors who started me on the human factors journey, most notably Irving Streimer and Harry Snyder. Special thanks also to my wife, Carol, for her continued love and support throughout the years.

—Bill Muto

Table of Contents

Tables

Figures

Preface

From its early days, human factors has focused on the identification and prevention of human error. And yet, most human factors practitioners have not had to deal with the formal techniques, tools, and language associated with risk analysis and risk management. On the other hand, non-human-factors practitioners who are well versed in risk management are often at a loss when dealing with human error.

While most references on risk management concentrate on failure of mechanical and electrical systems, this book concentrates on identifying and controlling human error in systems. It is intended as a user guide to the most common risk management tools that are applicable to a wide variety of products and systems. Among the many risk management tools mentioned, we discuss and illustrate with case studies two of the most-used methodologies: failure modes and effects analysis (FMEA) and fault tree analysis (FTA). Although our case studies focus on medical devices, the methods discussed are applicable to many products and systems, including those in industries such as transportation, nuclear power generation, aerospace, consumer products, and health care.

The book offers useful tools for user interface designers, human factors practitioners, engineers, quality and regulatory personnel, product regulators, and product development managers, as well as serving as an instructional guide for faculty and students. Novices with no experience, those who are knowledgeable about general risk management methods but have not applied them to use-related risk, and experts who need a refresher about using related assessment and control methods will benefit.

We realize that the term "human error" in the book title is disdained by many human factors practitioners because it is often used to imply that human errors belong to a class of immutable phenomena for which nothing can be done to prevent them. Worse yet, the term is often used to blame individuals as being the cause of an accident or incident when an error is identified. In contrast, we as human factors practitioners strive to identify opportunities when errors or their effects could be eliminated or reduced using proper analysis techniques and good design. In recent years, regulators and designers of medical products have used a more neutral term—"use error"—instead of "human error" or "user error." In this book, we have adopted the same convention. We use "human error" in the title only because it is more easily recognized by many prospective readers.

In the United States, the Food and Drug Administration (FDA) has special preferences for the application of risk management tools for medical devices that differ to some degree from the more traditional risk management techniques. We discuss these differences, but we do not focus on the agency's risk management philosophies to the exclusion of the traditional methods. At the same time, we alert the reader about the special considerations needed for filing medical device regulatory applications.

Acknowledgments

We acknowledge the excellent guidance and editorial advice of Phil Kortum on the final versions of this book and early guidance from Frank Durso on the initial drafts, which he convinced us to write. We also owe enormous appreciation to Lois Smith for her extraordinary editing efforts. We are sincerely thankful for our outside draft reviewers, Bob North, Kevin Cluff, and Changwon Son. Finally, thanks to Relyence Corporation for its support and use of its excellent software tool, Relyence Fault Tree.

1 Introduction and Overview of Risk Management for Use-Related Hazards

Risk management as a concept has been around since ancient times. It is reported that Julius Caesar, the emperor of Rome, first discussed the concept of risk and its prediction in the planning for battle. Caesar is reported to have said, "*Quod malum posset futurum,*" or, "What is bad will come to pass." This was qualified by other accredited statements, immortalized by Shakespeare, that "The fault, dear Brutus, is not in our stars, but in ourselves." That is, we can analyze the risk of something going badly and potentially do something about it (Shore, 1994).

The common definition of "risk" in "risk management" combines the likelihood of something going wrong with the severity of the negative event. *Merriam-Webster* defines risk as follows:

1. possibility of loss or injury: PERIL
2. someone or something that creates or suggests a hazard
3. a. the chance of loss or the perils to the subject matter of an insurance contract *also*: the degree of probability of such loss
   b. a person or thing that is a specified hazard to an insurer
   c. an insurance hazard from a specified cause or source
4. the chance that an investment (such as a stock or commodity) will lose value

In the realm of safety (that is, freedom from harm), risk is defined as the likelihood of a fault (usually a negative event such as a malfunction, error, or other failure) causing harm combined with the severity of the harm. Use-focused risk management specifically examines faults that are associated with human behavior in the form of task-based interactions with systems, usually of a safety-critical nature.

To put the concept of risk in perspective, it can be useful to think about real-life situations resulting in various levels of risk. Here are a few examples.

- Death or serious injury could occur when a commercial airplane crashes. Yet because crashes are relatively rare, we view their probability or likelihood to be low, so most would say that commercial flying is relatively low risk.
- Riding in a passenger car can also result in serious injury or death. But because we know that the likelihood of a car crash is much more likely than an airplane crash, we say that riding in a car has higher risk than flying. Despite that fact, even though it is well known that the drive to the airport is riskier than the flight itself, many people still have an irrational fear of flying because of the catastrophic nature of a crash at high speed and from high altitude.
- Getting hit by lighting can result in severe injury or death. If in a protected shelter, we consider the likelihood of being struck to be low and the overall risk to be low. However, if we stand outside in a flat field during a thunderstorm, the risk seems much higher because the likelihood of being struck has increased.

People are often surprised to see statistics reflecting the relative risks of various activities. Many times, risk perceptions do not match the data. Makary and Daniel (2016) compare death rates of activities relative to the number of encounters for each fatality, ranging from highly risky bungee jumping and mountain climbing to much lower risk levels associated with train and air travel and nuclear power generation.

This book provides a formal framework for conducting this kind of analysis of risk, with a focus on the role of human-system interactions in estimating and managing risk. In this book, you will find detailed explanations of methods that are applicable to safety-critical systems. The primary methods relevant to risk management center on performing three main functions: risk analysis, risk evaluation, and risk control. The case study examples are taken from the medical device domain and include an automatic external defibrillator and a blood glucose meter.

Risk management is a process. As shown in Figure 1.1, the first step is risk analysis, which identifies the hazards, hazardous situations, and possible harm that could occur. Risk analysis involves using existing data sources to estimate the likelihood of occurrence of faults and the severity of the harms that could result. From this analysis the level of risk is estimated by logically or mathematically combining likelihood of occurrence (frequency) estimates and resulting severity of harm. (See more on this in Chapter 3.) This combination of frequency and severity is described as the "risk index" or risk level. Be aware that it is common for some to use "risk analysis" as a synonym for "risk management," but strictly speaking, they are not equivalent. Risk analysis is a subset of risk management.

The second step in the risk management process is risk evaluation, in which the enterprise decides on its tolerability for risk and analyzes options. These first two steps are called "risk assessment." The third step is "risk control," in which risk mitigations are introduced and evaluated. Typically, all risk cannot be controlled or eliminated completely; what remains is called "residual risk." The acceptability of residual risk typically depends

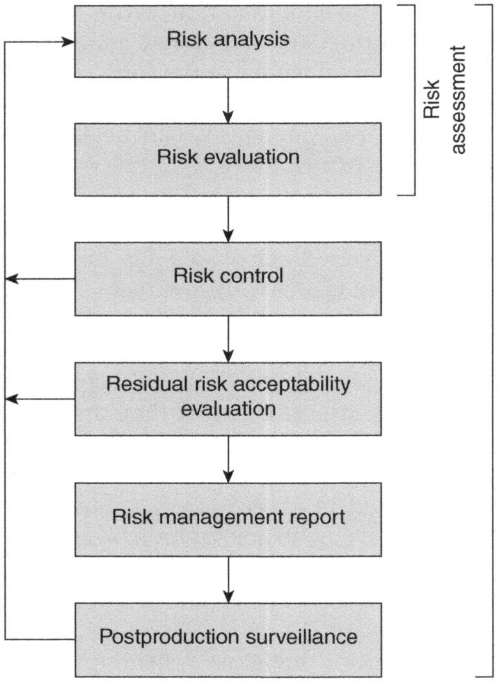

Figure 1.1. Relationships among the elements of risk management.

on what is found in doing a comparison or trade-off weighing the benefit of the product or system against the residual risk.

Where Can the Risk Management Process Be Applied?

You can apply risk management to many areas. Four main categories are often described.

- *Design of a product or system*—risk management (analysis, evaluation, and control) applied to the individual components of a design and the overall system.
- *Use of a product or system*—risk management applied to the tasks and scenarios of use of a product or system by a user.
- *Manufacturing process for a product*—risk management applied to the process of manufacturing a product or system and all the steps and quality control points in that process.
- *Enterprise*—risk management applied to economical or project-related failures and the consequences to the business enterprise, such as loss of revenue, project delay, or tarnishing of a brand image.

In this book, we focus on use-related risk due to human factors considerations of the users and their interaction with products and systems. Although our case study examples are from the medical device domain, you can apply the methods and techniques to many other domains, including aviation, ground transportation, power generation, mining, construction, home appliances, law enforcement, and military systems, among many others. We will be using the term "use error" instead of "user error" or "human error" to avoid blaming the user for errors. The goal of risk analysis is to investigate the root causes of error related to use, including faulty user interface design. "Use error" is intended to be a neutral term and is preferred by regulators and user interface designers in the health care and medical device areas.

Analysis of Benefit Versus Risk

To lower risk level, mitigations need to be applied—including modifications to the user interface design—in an iterative manner until the risk is reduced as far as reasonably practicable. A point is reached when it is not feasible or practical to apply additional mitigations to further reduce risk, leaving residual risk. If the manufacturer's predefined level of acceptability of residual risk is below that threshold, the product likely will be launched. But often in the final analysis of any risk management process, the enterprise must decide if the trade-offs between the benefits of a product or system outweigh the residual risk. Residual risk is inevitable because of the very difficult challenge in designing a product or system that is completely free of faults or risks.

A related concept is called "as low as reasonably practicable," or ALARP. ALARP is described in ISO 14971:2019, *Medical Devices—Application of Risk Management to Medical Devices*, section D, 8.1, as follows.

> After a particular risk control option or set of control options have been applied, there are three possible results:
>
> a. the residual risk exceeds the manufacturer's criterion for risk acceptability and the project is cancelled; unless subsequent Benefit/Risk analysis shows that the benefit compared to the residual risk justifies launching the product.

b. the residual risk is acceptable because it is so small as to be negligible or
c. the residual risk is between the two states specified in a) and b); for these risks the residual risk is acceptable for the option that reduces the risk to the lowest practicable level, bearing in mind the benefits resulting from its acceptance and taking into account the costs of any further reduction. This is the ALARP concept. (ISO, 2019)

The Food and Drug Administration has issued guidances on factors for us to consider when performing an analysis of benefit versus risk for medical products (FDA, 2012, 2016b). The main points are that benefits can be a number of quantifiable variables, including cure rates, extended life, and improved quality of life (e.g., less pain, more mobility); you can probably think of many more attainable personal benefits. You would then compare these benefits with the residual risk achieved through ALARP analysis, which could also be a number of quantifiable variables, including impact of side effects (e.g., increased frequency of heart attacks, strokes, cancer, and reduced ability to drive). ALARP gives us a handle on the levels of residual risk, whereas benefit-versus-risk analysis allows us to evaluate what might be acceptable levels of residual risk that appear to be above a manufacturer's predefined threshold. Benefit–risk analysis would not need to include costs due to economic or technical feasibility (e.g., making the product unaffordable or too complex to be used effectively), but ALARP would include an analysis of costs and resources—that is, practicality.

An example of this type of analysis is that there is approximately a 3% chance of death while undergoing coronary artery bypass graph (CABG) surgery, but the benefit is avoiding a high likelihood of death from future heart attacks if the coronary artery blockages are not eliminated. Therefore, the residual risk of death (3%) from CABG surgery is acceptable given the significant benefit that can be achieved. For other processes or products, a 3% residual risk of death would be unacceptable if the benefit were not as great as that for CABG surgery.

Another example is the use of an automatic external defibrillator (AED) by a lay (nonexpert) user to shock a heart that is in fibrillation back to normal rhythm, which is typically successful only 15% of the time. This means there is an extraordinarily high failure rate of 85%. But a life is saved when such AED use is successful, which is obviously a huge benefit. So, we can say the benefit versus risk is acceptable for AEDs—and indeed, they are ubiquitous in public places like airports, schools, and sporting facilities.

A final example is the use of a nasal spray to administer naloxone, a highly effective antidote for an opioid overdose. The naloxone nasal spray is close to 100% effective in reversing opioid overdoses if administered correctly in the first 5 minutes after an overdose. The administration of the spray was estimated to be about 58% successful (after training) in one simulated use study that compared nasal spray with autoinjector drug delivery (Edwards et al., 2015). Other studies have reported higher success rates for the nasal spray.

Even at the lower estimated success rate of 58%, the 42% failure rate for proper administration of the spray seems unreasonably high. However, when you consider the spray's overwhelming (near 100%) reversal rate of lethal opioid overdosing, which is otherwise almost always fatal, it shows a remarkably large benefit-to-risk comparison evaluation. That is why naloxone nasal spray can be obtained in the United States and around the world.

Rationale for Risk Management

Our primary motivation for engaging in risk management is to identify the elements of a product or system design that can lead to user or system harm and to analyze and then determine what can be done to mitigate against these negative outcomes. It is a systematic attempt to predict system faults that can lead to failure, harm, or serious injury and to provide means to prevent such harm. Failure to perform risk management obviates the opportunity to prevent possible systems failures that can have serious negative consequences. You and your team should do this type of analysis systematically, comprehensively, and with adequate attention to detail.

The high-level process for risk analysis is illustrated in Figure 1.1. Details about the methodologies are provided in Chapters 2 and 3. In the following discussion, we will cover the methods at a high level so you can better understand the overall process flow before getting into the precise details.

What are the typical hazards that you might analyze and investigate? Of course, the hazards that you examine will depend on your particular problem, product, or situation. The following overall list is adapted from the FDA guidance on human factors for medical devices (FDA, 2016a) and ISO 14971 (ISO, 2019).

- Biological hazards (e.g., under- or overdose of therapies such as drugs, allergic reactions, bio-incompatibility, and infection)
- Mechanical hazards (e.g., crash, crushing, kinetic or potential energy from a moving object)
- Chemical hazards (e.g., toxic chemicals)
- Thermal hazards (e.g., burns from high-temperature components)
- Electrical hazards (e.g., electrical shock, electromagnetic interference)
- Radiation hazards (e.g., ionizing and nonionizing)
- Enterprise hazards (e.g., project failure costs and lost time and revenues)
- Operational hazards (e.g., use errors, functional failures)
- Information hazards (e.g., labeling, operating instructions, quick-reference guides that are inferior and do not provide useful information).

To begin, you would list the appropriate use-related hazards, which you would get from brainstorming and investigating historical information from a variety of sources. Those might include

- user complaints,
- recalls,
- adverse events reports and databases typically maintained by regulators,
- results from previous usability evaluations, and
- review of the relevant literature on user behavior for similar user interactions.

Next, you would sort and then prioritize the harms that can result from the use-related hazards. The foundation for this prioritization results from performing and documenting a comprehensive task analysis to understand the user task flow. (See Stuster, 2019, a user guide in this HFES series on the topic of task analysis.) The task and subtask statements that you derive from the task analysis serve as inputs to common tools such as failure modes and effects analysis, or FMEA, and fault tree analysis (FTA), which are described in Chapters 3 and 4 and illustrated in much greater detail in the case study in Chapter 5. We often use these tools to perform the risk and harm prioritization.

The prioritized risks are used to guide the iterative design of the product and to inform you about what needs to be evaluated in a usability assessment, which ideally includes usability testing (see Chapter 3 and the later discussion) and reviews by user interface experts. The early usability tests are called "formative tests," and they serve the purpose of evaluating the user interface as well as the effectiveness of the risk mitigations.

You would feed the early formative usability test results back to the risk analysis to determine if the assessment of risk can be reduced to an acceptable level. This involves the benefit versus risk trade-off and ALARP concepts that we described earlier. If the residual risk is not acceptable, then further work on improving the user interface and labeling must be pursued and the subprocess repeated until the residual risk is acceptable and can be justified based on the benefit–risk trade-off.

In the next step, you would assess whether the mitigations introduced new hazards, which might come about through the introduction of new tasks or undesired outcomes. If new hazards are likely, they would need to be addressed through the process until they could be brought to an acceptable level.

The final step is for you to validate the user interface through final summative usability testing of what would be the final interface design. This is the last check to ensure that the design mitigations address and control the prioritized risks. If this summative validation fails (i.e., if more use errors are observed that could be further mitigated), then you must reenter the process at the stage of implementing new risk mitigations and controls in the user interface. At all steps in the iterative design process, any risk management tools, such as FMEAs and FTAs, should be incremented and updated.

Hierarchy of Risk Mitigation and Control

Risk mitigation and control is ideally done using a hierarchy. The best control of risk is to design out the causes of failure; for example, by designing a more intuitive user interface that will not lead to use error failures, particularly on critical tasks. The least powerful mitigations involve risk communication, which you would typically find in operating instructions and labeling. The risk mitigation desired hierarchy is as follows.

- Design out the likelihood of use error in the user interface (e.g., provide an intuitive user interface that is easy to learn and use).
- Guard against the use error (via protective measures such as safety guards and interlocks).
- Warn about the use error (through, for example, warning screens or alarms).

After exhausting those options, we would mitigate through risk communication mechanisms such as

- including risk information in instructions for use (IFU) and labeling (information for safety),
- including risk information in training courses and related product materials, or
- modifying the intended use claim (exclude certain user groups or use environments in the labeling).

Table 1.1. Risk Mitigations for Use of a Coffee Maker

Example of Mitigations in the Hierarchy **Product:** Coffee maker **Use error:** User inadvertently turns off coffee maker when intending to start the brewing process. **Root cause:** The Power on/off button is adjacent to the Brew start button, and users sometimes select the wrong button when trying to begin the brewing process.	
Type of Mitigation	**Description**
Design out the use error	Place the on/off button on the opposite side of the coffee maker faceplate from the Start Brewing button, so that they are far apart.
Guard against the use error	Put a hinged guard over the on/off button that must be lifted out of the way to use the on/off Power button.
Warn against the use error	Place a message on the coffee maker screen asking if the user is sure they want to turn off the coffee maker.
Include directions in the instructional materials (IFU)	Put a warning in the IFU that the two buttons are near each other and urge caution in using them to avoid inadvertently turning off the coffee maker.
Include directions in the training materials	Direct users to an online video showing how to use the coffee maker and pointing out the proximity of the two buttons and the need to be careful when using them.

Table 1.1 illustrates the hierarchy of mitigations for a simple coffee maker. The use error illustrated is inadvertently turning it off when the intention is to start the brewing process. The mitigations range from good design at the top to the very weak and often ineffective mitigations of user instructions and training.

Labeling or information for safety such as instructions for use and training are generally considered a less reliable form of risk mitigation, mostly because users often do not read or remember these materials, or the items may not even be available at the point of use. Many factors must be aligned and met for labeling to be successful for both the user and the label design itself. For labeling to be successful, all of the following actions need to be satisfied by both the user and the label design.

- Label is detected.
- Label is read.
- Label is comprehended.
- Decision to act must be undertaken.
- Decision must be complied with.

An important part of the user's decision to comply with a warning label involves the trade-off between perceived risk and the cost of compliance. Perceived risk is what the user personally believes is the actual risk, as opposed to the stated risk. The cost of compliance is what the user perceives as the amount of effort needed to comply with the warning label. We can illustrate this trade-off with two examples.

High voltage warning sign: User complies with the warning sign that death or serious injury can result from contact with an outside high-voltage electrical transformer that is protected by a high fence with barbed wire at the top. User complies because they perceive the risk of electrocution to genuinely be high and the cost of compliance low, since a great deal of effort would be needed to scale the high fence and very little effort is needed to stay outside the fence.

> **SURGEON GENERAL WARNING:**
> Cigarette somoking can cause lung cancer and heart disease.

Cigarette smoking warning label: Many users ignore the warning about the dangers of lung cancer or heart disease on a pack of cigarettes. Often, smokers perceive low personal risk because they believe they are immune to the common health effects of smoking and that it applies only to other people. The cost of compliance with the warning is very high, because the smoking habit and addiction to nicotine are powerful, and it takes a great deal of effort to stop smoking to comply with the label warning.

The overarching reason for this systematic approach to assessing risk is to understand at some level of detail that we want to improve product usability for tasks that could lead to personal harm or project (enterprise) failure. At the end of the day, we want to reduce, to the extent possible, either the severity of the harm or its likelihood (as described earlier in the ALARP concept) or both.

Another consideration for risk involves general usability. If that is poor, users may find unsafe workarounds and short-cuts and bypass safety-related aspects of a user interface, rendering the overall design unsafe—the relevant analogy being "death by a thousand small cuts." A single user interface design fault may cause harm, but the totality of minor design faults could have the undesired effect of compromising safe use.

Common Risk Management Tools and Methods

A number of risk management tools are available for analyzing and controlling risk. As we mentioned previously, the most commonly used tool is failure modes and effects analysis. There are three typical types.

- *Design FMEA* focuses on the components of a design, such as hardware elements.
- *Use or application FMEA* (or uFMEA) focuses on tasks by users when interacting with the device or system.
- *Process FMEA* focuses on the steps in a process, such as manufacturing steps.

Table 1.2. Example of a Risk Chart for Determining the Risk Index Value

Probability of Occurrence	Hazard and Resulting Harm Severity		
	Major	**Moderate**	**Minimal**
Probable	High	High	Medium
Occasional	High	Medium	Low
Rare	Medium	Low	Low
Improbable	Low	Low	Low

Some analysts also specify a system-level FMEA, in which these three types are integrated, sometimes with the addition of specialized FMEAs, such as service and maintenance activities, environmental interactions, and system integration activities.

FMEAs usually take the form of a table, in which each row is a failure needing to be analyzed (e.g., a product component, user task, or process step). The columns can vary, but you would include these:

- fault description,
- probability estimate of the fault occurring and causing harm,
- description of the effect of the fault and possibly the resulting hazardous situation,
- description of the harm,
- assessment of the severity of the harm, and
- risk index, derived from the combination of fault probability of occurrence and severity of harm (derived from a risk chart).

Table 1.2 shows an example of a risk chart with one axis depicting the probability of harm and the second depicting the severity of harm. The cells at the intersection of each axis are the risk index values, which take the descriptors of high, medium, or low risk level. This example uses qualitative descriptions for the axes and resultant risk indexes. The probabilities would usually have descriptive parameters (e.g., how often during the normal life of product use), and your harm severities might vary from major (death or permanent injury), to moderate (serious but not permanent injury), to minimal (minor or no discomfort).

Other risk charts could be semiquantitative and use numerical scales whose values you would multiply for probability and severity. We will cover all this in much more detail in Chapters 2 and 3.

In the United States, the FDA considers harm to also include compromised medical care, which would involve having to give the user additional medical therapy because of the use error, such as prescribing an antibiotic medication or applying a cast for a broken bone. The level of compromised medical care would be part of the severity level of the harm.

As we noted earlier, fault tree analysis is another commonly used tool. As described in more detail in Chapter 4, its value is in helping you understand complex combinations of events that can lead to hazards and faults. FTA takes the form of an inverted graphical tree, with the fault at the top and the branches below it showing the logical combination of events, such as use errors or environmental conditions that can lead to the fault. (An example is shown in Figure 4.1, page 40.)

In later chapters—for example, Chapter 6 (the blood glucose meter case study) and Chapter 7 (additional considerations)—we will discuss closely related tools that some regulators (like the FDA) require, such as use-related risk analysis (URRA) and use error risk analysis (UERA).

The FDA mandates the identification of "critical tasks" in which a use error during performance of the task can lead to serious harm. These critical tasks are the focus of attention for risk reduction through product redesign and validation testing. In the URRA, the focus is solely on severity of harm, and most notably, the probability of use error leading to harm is not even considered. That is because the FDA is highly skeptical about the reliability of probability estimates of human behavior. Nevertheless, we strongly believe that probability of occurrence estimates (even if very rough and approximate) are absolutely necessary in determining whether remaining (residual) risk after mitigations is acceptable. That is because risk reduction is much more often achieved by reducing the likelihood of use error than by lowering the severity of harm. The severity level is almost always an inherent attribute of the design space that cannot be influenced by the development team.

We believe there is a place for both URRA and traditional use error FMEA (or uFMEA) in risk management, with the careful and judicious use of conservative estimates of likelihood or probability of occurrence for harm.

Methods to Predict Use Errors

The Venn diagram in Figure 1.2 illustrates the complementary nature of usability testing and risk analysis. Usability testing is a mainstay of human factors, because it involves observation of the task-based performance of a representative user. Typically, usability testing involves the user performing essential and critical tasks while a moderator and observers record the success or failure under simulated use conditions that are representative of the actual real-world use environment.

Usability testing is empirical, because you would observe and record actual user behavior. Testing is typically done with small samples sizes (e.g., 15 subjects per distinct user group). It provides an excellent opportunity for us to see users in action. On the other hand, risk analysis as described in this book is an analytical process in which we engage subject matter experts to identify and attempt to predict the types of use error failures that might occur.

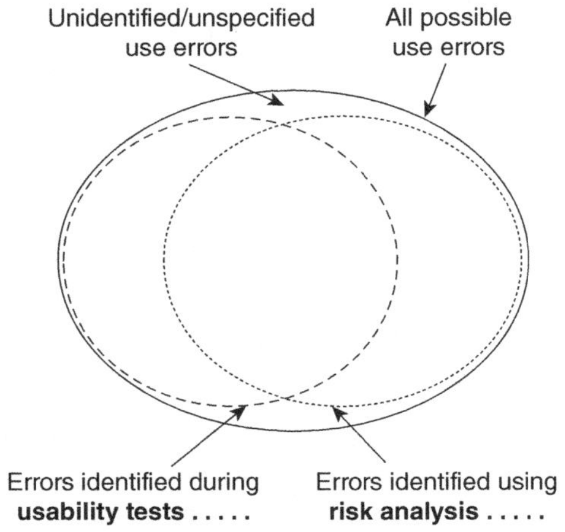

Figure 1.2. Venn diagram comparing use errors identified by either risk analysis or usability tests.

In the ideal world, the two circles representing usability testing and risk analysis in Figure 1.2 would overlap completely, and both methods would capture the same use errors. However, in reality, each method is not perfect, and we will have false positive and false negative outcomes for each. The expert predictions of some use errors may not be observed in the usability tests results, and conversely, use errors may be seen in the usability tests that our experts did not foresee in the analytical risk analysis.

Sampling error can explain the failure to observe some of the use errors in usability tests, and experts may not always have sufficient information to predict all use errors. Also, as shown in Figure 1.2, some possible use errors are missed by both methods and may become apparent only after a product is launched and postmarket surveillance records these instances of unanticipated use errors.

Nonetheless, both methods—analytical risk analysis and empirical usability testing—are complementary and offer a better chance of use error prediction when we employ them together. That is what regulators want us to do for medical products. This book focuses on the risk management process, and another book in this series (Kortum, 2016) focuses on usability assessment.

The Relationships Among Hazards, Hazardous Situations, Harm, and Risk

A final foundational thought on risk management concepts and tools is the importance of understanding the relationships among the risk management concepts of hazard, sequence of events, hazardous situations, harm, and risk. For reference, here are the concepts.

- *Hazard*: potential source of harm.
- *Sequence of events*: a series of events that occur.
- *Hazardous situation*: circumstance in which people, property, or the environment are exposed to one or more hazards.
- *Harm*: physical injury or damage to health of people or damage to property or the environment.
- *Risk*: combination of the probability of occurrence of harm and the severity of that harm.

The relationship starts with a hazard that, through a sequence of events, can lead to a hazardous situation. We can label the probability of exposure to the hazardous situation as P_1. The probability of the hazardous situation leading to harm is P_2. The product of P_1 and P_2 ($P_1 \times P_2$) is the resultant probability of harm for any given fault or use error.

Every harm has a severity level, which, when combined with the probability of harm, results in a risk, which may have a value we label as "risk level" or "risk index." Some refer to this erroneously as "risk priority number" (RPN). RPN traditionally refers to the product of three terms: "probability," "severity," and "detection of a fault." Instead of using the third term, some analysts use the term "estimate of likelihood of mitigation control success." Hazards associated with high RPNs would be higher priority, and that would warrant mitigation.

To illustrate the relationship between hazard, hazardous situation, and harm, we offer an example involving the hazard of encountering a shark. The hazardous situation results from the sequence of events in which a hungry shark is present and a person is swimming nearby. The harm is that the person is severely injured or killed when the shark attacks them. P_1 is the probability that there is a hazardous situation consisting of a hungry shark and a nearby swimmer. P_2 is the probability that this hazardous situation leads to harm to the swimmer. $P_1 \times P_2$ is the resulting probability that a shark attacks and harms the swimmer.

Now that we have explained some of the concepts and motivation for risk management, in the next chapter we will detail the more common methodologies that are used.

2 Preparation for Risk Management

Two activities are needed to start your risk analysis. The first is the formation of a human factors risk analysis team. The second is the preparation of a preliminary hazard analysis. In this chapter, we also introduce a hypothetical project that will be used to illustrate the risk management process: an automatic external defibrillator (AED).

Form a Team

Formation of a team is critical in conducting and managing risk management activities.

Why is a team necessary to perform risk management?

The involvement of a team enables multiple points of view that can aid in the creation of a complete and well-balanced analysis. Stamatis (1995) suggests that the risk management process acts as a "catalyst to stimulate the interchange of ideas between functional areas."

Often the demands of shorter schedules, minimal staffing requirements, and lower costs may motivate some organizations to assign the risk analysis activities to one or two individuals. The problem with assigning only one or two people is that their perspectives will be more limited than the broader perspectives that multiple team members' knowledge and experiences can bring to crucial risk management steps such as brainstorming. The lack of multiple team members may limit how well the analyses represent the real world, increasing the likelihood that the risk analysis will fail to identify faults that should have been identified or that risk levels will be under- or overestimated.

Equally important, perhaps, is that a single person (or two) is likely to have less influence (and credibility) than a group when needing to convince design teams or management that identified risks are legitimate and actions are required to mitigate them. Reviewers of the work may unintentionally be dismissive of a one- or two-person report and disregard or downgrade identified risks. Consequently, we recommend that careful attention be paid to the formation of a team.

Team Leader

The group will need a team leader, who will be responsible for managing the team's basic operations. Your leader's main role is to facilitate the risk management process rather than act as the key decision maker. The team leader will have to be well versed in the risk management process and able to lead team activities. The leader's responsibilities should include

- setting up and running meetings,
- leading the meetings to ensure they run efficiently and remove any roadblocks to success,
- ensuring that team representation and resources are adequate,
- ensuring the timely and accurate management of the risk analysis (e.g., FMEA) records, and
- communicating progress and issues to management.

Team Size

A team should be large enough to ensure sufficient representation of key stakeholders. Although one or two members are not enough to represent key stakeholders, attempting to include all possible stakeholders can result in a team that is too large and unwieldy. Such a team is likely to consume more time and resources with little or no incremental benefit. We recommend that a team consist of about five core members, who can rely on a small network of supporting members. The supporting members need attend meetings only on request.

Team Composition

The success of your team will largely depend on the expertise and dedication of the people assigned to it. To maximize the probability of success, you should select your team members based on the following considerations rather than merely on people's availability.

- *Knowledge of the risk analysis process.* Prior experience with risk analysis will enable the person to be a contributing team member and minimize the learning curve.
- *Knowledge of the system or device to be analyzed.* Most products are based on "predicate" (previously developed or marketed) devices or systems. For development of devices based on predicates, it is prudent to select team members with knowledge of and experience with the same product. For development of devices that do not have predicates, it is beneficial to include team members who are familiar with products that have similar working domains, user profiles, and use environments.
- *Direct or indirect ownership of the problem ("stakeholders").* Any development project involves people from a range of disciplines, who will be responsible for the specification, design, evaluation, and distribution of the product. In medical device companies, stakeholders for use-related analyses could include persons from the following disciplines:
    - human factors engineering (with knowledge of users, user interface design, user behavior, usability test methodologies, etc.),
    - hardware engineering (knowledge of systems, mechanical engineering),
    - software engineering (knowledge of software and users), and
    - training/user documentation (knowledge of users and current training methods).

Other individuals may be invited to participate on an ad hoc basis to provide insight into specific issues. For example, medical affairs personnel (typically including people with clinical knowledge and experience) are essential when identifying and classifying the severity of hazards and resulting harms early in the process, but they may not be required throughout the entire process. Service personnel may be essential when dealing with on-site maintenance or troubleshooting issues. Other personnel may include representatives from regulatory, quality assurance, risk management, and safety.

Practical Considerations and Expectations

It is important to note that risk assessments represent the collective opinion of a team and that reaching consensus can be difficult sometimes. Different teams will create different final results. In our experience, working through the first few hazards may take one or two full meetings. Do not despair—the team will usually find a rhythm.

Adding new members to the team can be initially challenging when a newcomer disagrees with the team's ratings. The challenge can stem from differences in the new member's aversion to risk or their progress on the learning curve. Similar differences can occur on a large scale when a team is required to review analyses by a different team that may have been done several years earlier. The team should avoid the temptation to immediately overhaul the previous analysis. Both situations could benefit from careful review of previous team assumptions and methods to "calibrate" team judgments, such as the Delphi method, described in Chapter 7.

Identifying Hazards—Preliminary Hazard Analysis

Now that you have formed your team, your first activity is to perform a preliminary hazard analysis (PHA). The hazard analysis is intended to identify potential hazards of the device. As described in Chapter 1, hazards are conditions that can lead to hazardous situations that have potential for harm, which is defined as physical injury or damage to the health of people or damage to property or the environment. Harm can also be nonsafety or business related. Business-related risks such as loss of sales and reduced customer satisfaction should not be part of a safety-focused analysis.

You should perform the hazard analysis as early in the life cycle as possible, starting at the concept phase. The hazards you identify at this time should be essentially the same for all risk analysis teams, so this analysis could be developed in common and/or shared among groups.

There are two reasons for performing a hazard analysis early in the life cycle. First, any risk analysis (design or use error) for the system will need to include identified hazards. Second, the earlier hazards are recognized, the more likely that countermeasures (also known as "mitigations," "methods of control," or "modes of control") for these hazards will be incorporated into the design of the product.

If the hazard analysis finds that the device cannot harm the patient or users in any conceivable use scenario, and if the device has been determined to have no hazards or hazards with only minor severity, the hazard analysis and subsequent risk analyses should reflect these findings. That is more likely to be true for what the FDA designates as Class I (low-risk) medical devices and some limited Class II devices.

A hazard could be caused by device failure, use error, or both. However, a hazard analysis is not intended as a means to identify the causes or circumstances leading to hazards. To identify hazards, your team will need to conduct brainstorming sessions, augmented by reviews of information for the same type of device or similar devices from the company's documents, including complaint records and company call center records.

ISO 14971:2019, an international standard for risk management of medical devices, categorizes hazards into three types: (a) energy-related hazards (e.g., electrical, mechanical, radiation), (b) biological and chemical hazards, and (c) functionality and information-related hazards. The first two categories encompass traditional safety concerns related to possible harm caused by the device itself or by possible exposure to chemicals or biological materials. The third category is where many—perhaps most—of the human factors concerns reside. This category includes safety-related issues regarding functionality, usability, information, communication, and labeling. As mentioned in Chapter 1, the FDA uses similar categories for classifying hazards.

Where can we find publicly available records of medical device issues that can be used for our risk management analysis?

Medical device reporting (MDR) is a postmarket surveillance system that the FDA uses to monitor device performance, detect potential device-related safety issues, and perform benefit–risk assessments of these products. Manufacturers, users at facilities where these devices are employed, and importers are required to report adverse events and device problems to the FDA. Likewise, health care professionals and other device users are encouraged to submit reports about adverse events that may be associated with a device, as well as use errors and therapeutic failures. The MDR system offers information that provides insight into design, manufacturing, or use-related issues that helps to improve patient safety.

Reports for adverse events and product problems have been cataloged in an online database called Manufacturer and User Facility Device Experience (MAUDE). Computerized searches of MAUDE can be conducted across all devices for which incidents have been reported in the 10 years prior to the date of search (FDA, 2020a).

Adverse event descriptions are catalogued by event number, device identifier, event type, manufacturer, date, and brand name, all of which can be used as search parameters. You can import this information into spreadsheet programs for conducting automated searches for selected parameters or key words. Search filtering is useful or necessary when events can number in the hundreds or thousands.

The event descriptions are raw, textual, often lengthy narrations of events in which the situation and problems are reported for a specific device. In many event descriptions, no causes or resolutions are given. Despite their shortcomings, these narrative descriptions can provide your team with useful inputs for the hazard analysis that you may not have thought of otherwise and will also be invaluable for brainstorming during the risk analysis process.

One of the first group of hazards identified for any medical devices should answer the question, "What harm can result from a device failing to do what it is supposed to do?" That is, if the device fails to perform its "critical" clinical function, also called "essential performance," in the language of medical device standards. Examples of hazards that have implications for direct or indirect harm to the patient include an infusion pump that fails to deliver the proper amount of fluids or medications in the prescribed period, a blood glucose meter that fails to provide an accurate reading, and an SO_2 (oxygen saturation) monitor that fails to accurately measure blood oxygen levels.

An infusion pump that delivers an improper amount of medication can cause direct harm to a patient due to underdose or overdose of a critical fluid. The SO_2 monitor and glucose meter can cause indirect harm when a caregiver treats a patient based on the devices' incorrect readings. An example list of hazards, hazardous situations, and their harms for an automatic injector is shown in Table 2.1.

Examination of other hazards will identify conditions that can lead to harm to the patient, caregiver, or bystander while preparing the device for use or during or after use. After the hazard analysis is complete, your team will perform the more common risk analysis techniques, such as the failure modes and effects analysis (FMEA) and fault tree analysis (FTA), described in the coming chapters.

Table 2.1. Examples of Possible Hazards, Harms, and Hazard-Related Use Scenarios for Various Devices

Hazard	Hazard-Related Use Scenario	Harm
Radiation energy	Physician accidentally activates unguarded fire control (UE). *Energy source operates (HS).* Energy source is directed at bystander.	Radiation burn
Sharp point of needle (infected needle)	After inserting intravenous catheter, physician places used unprotected needle onto hospital bed sheet (UE). Physician forgets to remove needle (UE). Orderly changes bed sheets. *Unprotected needle lying on hospital bed (HS).*	Infection caused by needle stick
Falling on hard floor	Hospital bed guardrail locking mechanism is difficult to engage. Nurse fails to recognize that the guardrail is not fully engaged (UE). *Guardrail not correctly engaged (HS).* Patient rolls onto side, pressing against guardrail. Guardrail drops and patient falls to floor.	Fractured hip
Incorrect output	Nurse inadvertently misconnects tubing of intravenous medication source to neuraxial access port (UE). The two different delivery routes use the same Luer connector. The nurse does not check the tubing connections from the medication source to the access port (UE). Intravenous medication is delivered to the patient's spinal nerve column.	Permanent paralysis
Incorrect output	The previous valid value of acceptable oxygen concentration in inspired gas mixture remains on the display, but the monitor requires recalibration. The failure to properly calibrate is not clearly indicated. The anesthetist fails to check the monitor calibration. The anesthetist believes that the oxygen supply is operating properly (UE). *Miscalibrated gas monitor displays a hazardous, incorrect value of oxygen concentration (HS).* The anesthetist delivers a hypoxic mixture to the patient.	Hypoxic brain injury
Incorrect output of drug (morphine)	A high volume of morphine is being administered to patient in a high-stress emergency care situation under low ambient lighting. The emergency physician needs to change the dose and cannot clearly read the display of the infusion pump. The emergency physician incorrectly inputs the concentration of the morphine infusion rate (UE). *Using an infusion pump that is difficult to read in this environment of use. Infusion pump delivers overdoes of morphine (HS).* Infusion pump delivers an overdose of morphine.	Respiratory arrest
Incorrect output of drug (insulin)	The patient (user) has poor vision. Unit of measure labels are not clear on the glucometer. There is poor ambient lighting in patient's home. Patient selects display of blood glucose in incorrect units and misreads current blood glucose level (UE). *Using a glucose meter that is difficult to read by a patient (HS).* Patient administers excessive amount of insulin.	Coma

Note: The use scenario description includes the sequence of events, including use errors and contributory factors that can lead to harm from a hazard with the hazardous situation. Underlining indicates the use error (UE). Italics indicate a hazardous situation (HS). Adapted from ISO 62366-1:2015.

3 Use Error Failure Modes and Effects Analysis (uFMEA)

Probably the most widely used risk analysis tool is failure modes and effects analysis (FMEA) and its close relative, failure modes effects and criticality analysis (FMECA). The basic objective of a device design FMEA is to answer these questions: "If a specified system component or subsystem fails, what is the effect on system performance or safety?" "What forms of control (also called 'mitigations,' 'recommended actions,' 'modes of control,' and 'methods of control') can be implemented to reduce the chance of failure or to reduce the severity of the effect?"

Rather than focusing on component or system failure, a use FMEA (uFMEA, also called "usability FMEA," "use error FMEA," and "human factors FMEA") focuses on user actions that deviate from expected or ideal performance. The goal of the analysis is to answer these questions (Israelski & Muto, 2012):

- If a user (anyone who may interact with the device, including a caregiver, health care provider, maintenance person, or the patient) fails to perform a task or performs it incorrectly, what is the effect on system performance or safety?
- What forms of control can be implemented to reduce the probability of the error or the severity of the effect?

Background

The steps you will use for conducting a uFMEA are basically the same as for conducting a system or device design FMEA. The difference is that it focuses on user task failure, the failure of a human operator to properly perform a designated task in a timely manner.

The overall process of developing a uFMEA is initiated with the aid of a task analysis. Enumerating the tasks associated with operating a system or device enables your team to brainstorm about potential use errors that could lead to each task failure. Each use error (considered a "failure mode" or "fault") is then rated in terms of (a) severity of the harm that can result, (b) probability of occurrence of harm caused by the use error, and (c) the resultant risk index, which is a combination of the severity and probability of the harm. The risk index is used to determine the priority for applying modes of control, or mitigations, to control the risk. For each of the items in which mitigations or a group of mitigations is applied, you will reevaluate the risk index. The process is iterated until all risks are reduced to acceptable levels.

Basic Steps in Performing uFMEA

In the rest of this chapter, we describe the procedural steps in performing a uFMEA. (In Chapter 5, we demonstrate the process of developing a uFMEA for a hypothetical medical device.) The steps are as follows.

1. Perform a task analysis.
2. Start a worksheet.
3. Brainstorm potential use errors (failure modes) for each task.
4. List potential effects of each use error/failure mode.
5. Assign severity ratings for the harm.

6. Estimate occurrence (probability) of use error leading to harm.
7. Assign a risk index.
8. Prioritize the failure modes/use errors by risk level.
9. List the method of control (mitigations) for each failure mode/use error.
10. Determine if new hazards have been introduced or if estimated risks for other hazards have been affected.
11. Assess the effect of mitigations on risk level (determine residual risk).
12. Assess whether or not residual risk levels are acceptable.
13. Repeat steps 9–12 until risks are at acceptable levels.

Step 1: Perform a Task Analysis

A task analysis is a detailed description of the tasks that users perform during preparation, operation, and relevant maintenance of a device or system. The description can be in graphical, tabular, or narrative form. Your analysis should cover the major tasks performed by the primary users of the product and will often include the following information:

- the person or persons performing the task,
- the task stimulus—signal or cue given to a user that initiates the task,
- the equipment or component used to perform the task,
- feedback to the user on performance of the task,
- required action (including decision-making), and
- the characteristics of the task output, including performance requirements.

There are many ways to document a task analysis. An example of a tabular hierarchical task analysis is shown in Table 3.1. (Figure 5.1 is an example of a graphical form.) See Stuster (2019) and Kirwan and Ainsworth (1992) for more thorough reviews of the topic.

Task analysis based on previous (predicate) devices. A primary source for task analysis is information derived from observing representative users of predicate devices. Observations performed by your team can provide insights into aspects of current user interfaces that may not be apparent otherwise.

When conducting a task analysis on a system whose user interface is based on a previous device or system, you'll find that one of the best sources of information is the device's instructional materials. A review of step-by-step instructions can provide the basis for a task analysis for the new device, even though the steps may differ between the previous system and the system being designed. Any new design elements, such as display functionality, control mechanisms, or interactions, can be extended from those of the previous device.

Task analysis for new systems with no predicate—early-phase task analysis. It may be challenging for a team to perform a task analysis on a system or user interface design that is in the planning or early design phase. In such instances, it can be highly beneficial to study work settings that employ similar devices or have similar tasks.

If the device under development has no predicate, a plan of study should focus on gathering information from similar devices and working environments. Among commonly recommended methodologies for gathering user needs and wants, task-related information, user-related problems, and the like is "contextual inquiry"—an information-gathering process with three main components: task analysis, user profiles, and use environment analysis.

Table 3.1. Example of a Hierarchical Task Description Analysis

Activity	Task	Subtask	Notes
Set up device	Calibrate unit	Connect sensor to load	
		Measure resistance	
		Adjust sensitivity control	If sensitivity cannot be adjusted, go to troubleshooting
	Check battery charge state	Read battery meter	
		Verify that reading is greater than 12 volts but less than 15 volts	If reading is not in range, go to battery charging activity
	Check mounting security	Tighten clamp until knob starts to slip	
		Gently pull down on unit to test for no movement	If movement detected, then readjust clamp
Start device	Initial start-up	Verify power is on	
		Check that sensor gauge reading is in starting range	
	Monitor status of reading	Check both sensor level and sensitivity readings for in-range readings	
Stop device	Press Stop button	Check for readings to return to zero	

From Israelski and Muto (2012).

Contextual inquiry may include the following activities for gathering vital information that can be used to identify what users need and want.

- Qualitative or quantitative observations, such as follow-around studies (shadowing), behavioral checklists completed by observers, and time-and-motion studies.
- Time slice sampling studies, in which users are observed and questioned at random times.
- Usability tests designed to understand tasks and user behaviors.
- Interviews and surveys (individual and focus groups).
- User-kept diaries and activity logs.

In the early concept phase, the details of the user interface may not yet be determined.

Updating task analysis and FMEA. You should update the task analysis and the associated uFMEA as the design of the system matures. Continue to update the FMEA throughout the design process, maintaining it as a "living document" until the design is finalized ("frozen"). The output of the FMEA should serve as input to the design teams and to human factors groups to guide risk-based formative usability evaluations. A version of the uFMEA could continue to exist and be updated as a tool to assess risks as part of postmarket surveillance.

Step 2: Start a Worksheet

Your team will document a uFMEA using a worksheet. The worksheet captures all the information about the FMEA and serves as an essential communication tool within the team and for other project entities, which can include engineering, marketing, training, user documentation, quality, and project management. It also serves as a primary subject for audits by regulatory agencies. The focus of any FMEA is failure modes; in uFMEAs, these modes will be the use error(s) or the use error scenarios.

Worksheets can vary widely in format. Your team can choose a format to suit your project based on project needs, company requirements, or internal standards. The most commonly used format is a tabular worksheet. A tabular FMEA is organized in rows and columns, in which each row describes an individual failure mode/use error and the columns display descriptors for each failure mode. Although some of the columns will be standard for any FMEA, the choice of column labels and overall layouts is often standardized within companies, divisions, or work groups. Table 3.2 is an example of FMEA worksheet column headers.

When you set up a tabular worksheet with a spreadsheet program such as Microsoft Excel™, many of the built-in utilities, (e.g., cutting, pasting, sorting, automatic numbering, searching, replacing, and spell checking) can be extremely useful for creating, organizing, editing, printing, and distributing the worksheet.

Another format, a FMEA form, is a document that contains the same information as the tabular worksheet. Rather than showing each failure mode as a row in a spreadsheet with descriptors in columns, you would enter the failure mode and its descriptors as fields on a one-page (or multipage) form. This format has several advantages, including ease of creation and ample space for complete descriptors and notes. A disadvantage of the form is that it can be more difficult to manage, especially when dealing with complex systems in which the FMEA line numbers could rise into hundreds (or more) of items.

FMEA software. You can also develop FMEAs using specialized software tools. Compared with manual methods using word-processing or spreadsheet programs, these tools are designed to increase group productivity and reduce effort in creating and managing the FMEAs. For example, Relyence FMEA (Relyence Corporation, https://relyence.com/products/fmea/) enables the worksheet data to be entered into preprogrammed blank fields on a form. After you enter the data, you can view and edit the FMEA in the familiar tabular (worksheet) format. The tool provides a number of features, including menu-based data entry (e.g., for severity and occurrence ratings), automatic calculation of risk indices, and automatic sorting.

Whichever tool your team uses for creating the FMEA worksheet, team meetings can be greatly enhanced by viewing the creation and editing process in real time. Real-time viewing can be done effectively with electronic projection for in-person meetings or by using internet-based virtual meeting software to enable remote viewing and participation.

Step 3: Brainstorm Potential Use Errors (Failure Modes) for Each Task

This is a crucial step in the FMEA process. For each of the tasks identified in the task analysis, the team will identify possible use errors—actions that deviate from expected or

Table 3.2. Example of Table Column Headers for a Human Factors FMEA Worksheet

FMEA Column Header	Description
1. Number	Reference number (usually sequential) given to each failure mode. This number is intended to stay with the failure mode, especially important when sorting the list.
2. Activity or use scenario	Task category.
3. Task	Task or subtask or step being performed provides context for failure mode.
4. Failure mode	Fault/use error or the sequence of events leading to the failure.
5. Potential effects of the failure	Description of the effects of the failure.
6. Hazardous situation	The situation that can lead to harm.
7. Harm	Description of the harm.
8. Severity	Severity of the harm.
9. Occurrence	Probability of the failure mode leading to the harm (initial rating—before mitigation is applied).
10. Risk level	Risk level based on severity and (initial) occurrence rating.
11. Recommended action	Description of action taken to mitigate the risk.
12. Revised occurrence	Probability of harm after mode of control is applied.
13. Revised risk level	Risk level after mitigation is applied.
14. Acceptance Level	Acceptance of revised risk level (e.g., acceptable, unacceptable, acceptable with justification). Note: Unacceptable would be entered only for interim analyses, not in the final FMEA.
15. Responsibility	These (optional) items are intended to be used to track action items and outcomes. They may be omitted if the action items are tracked separately by other project management mechanisms.
16. Target completion	
17. Action taken	
18. Effective date	
19. Reference for data that shows successful validation of risk mitigations	

optimal behavior. Team interactions for this phase should follow common brainstorming rules whereby inputs are recorded and the merits of the individual items are not debated until all ideas are captured.

The failure mode description can be as simple or complex as you deem necessary. In a simple case, a use error could lead directly to harm. For example, after using a syringe, the user forgets to deploy the needle guard and is punctured. In more complex cases, a failure mode may be described as a use scenario in which a failure is described in the presence of other environmental, task, or user conditions that potentially lead to harm. For instance, an infusion pump is mounted low on a pole in a dark room. The low mounting position results in an extreme vertical viewing angle that greatly reduces the display's contrast. While programming the pump, the user has difficulty reading the display and selects the wrong drug concentration level, resulting in a drug overdose.

All conceivable use errors should be documented for each task and subtask, which could include the following:

- use errors that may occur due to particular design attributes (called "design-induced errors");
- use errors that would be anticipated to follow predictable trends or patterns of behavior;
- common human mistakes or lapses of memory or attention—sources of "foreseeable human error" (some categorize such errors as "foreseeable misuse");
- errors observed in formative and summative usability studies; and
- use errors reported or observed on predicate devices or devices with similar user interfaces.

In addition, each distinct use environment should be considered. Different environments could lead to error-causing conditions. Consider also tasks performed by each user group. Differences in training, experience, and other demographic factors could increase the chance of use errors for some (e.g., use of a glucose monitor by lab technician vs. a layperson). Finally, refer to customer complaint data and medical device reports (MDRs).

Aids for brainstorming use errors. For teams not experienced in uFMEAs, it might be challenging to extract errors solely from task analysis information. Assistive aids for brainstorming errors include the use of error classifications and behavioral categories.

When you consider how a task could fail, one way to start is to think in terms of the types of errors. The following describes error classification schemes that could stimulate the brainstorming of potential errors.

Errors of omission and commission. The simplest error classification scheme is one that designates two types of errors: errors of omission and errors of commission. An error of omission is one in which a user fails to perform an action that should have been done. An error of commission is one in which a user performs an action that should not have been done (Wickens, Lee, Liu, & Gordon-Becker, 2004).

The following are examples of errors of omission that have happened in health care settings.

- A surgical nurse did not count the sponges used during a surgical procedure.
- The intake technician forgot to ask the patient if she had any allergies to medications.
- A medical technician failed to run "controls" to check the accuracy of a glucose meter.

These are examples of errors of commission:

- A caretaker reads the glucose meter with the display inverted (upside down). She reads a value of 501 mg/dL when the actual value is 105 mg/dL.
- A caregiver selects the wrong medication concentration from a menu of choices in the infusion pump.
- The pharmacist miscalculates the concentration of potassium needed to infuse a patient being treated for low potassium.

Error categories proposed by Reason: Slips, lapses, mistakes, and violations. Perhaps the best-known and most extensive error classification scheme has been proposed by Reason (1990). Based on the notion that an error is a failure to achieve a desired goal, Reason describes four basic types of errors: slips, lapses, mistakes, and violations. Slips and lapses are failures that occur during execution of a task rather than during planning or "formulation of intentions."

- A *slip* is an unintended commission error for a given action. In this context, a slip occurs when a person intends to perform a certain action, but the action is not executed as intended.
- A *lapse* is an unintended error of omission. In this case, a person fails to perform an action that was intended. Such errors are attributable to failures of memory.
- *Mistakes* are intended actions but are in error because the plan of action is incorrect or inappropriate to achieve the desired goal. Such errors involve failures in higher-level processes and the use of "rule-based" and "knowledge-based" information.
- A *violation* occurs when a person intentionally performs an action that is inappropriate or prohibited (by the manufacturer, organization, governing body, etc.).

Some medical device manufacturers have argued that users of medical devices are highly skilled and motivated professionals and that actions outside the prescribed use constitute "abnormal use" (belonging to the violation category). They further suggest that abnormal use constitutes extreme behaviors that are outside the manufacturer's responsibility and do not to need further consideration or mitigation. (See IEC 62366-1:2015 for further explanation.)

In recent years, a wide array of medical devices (e.g., blood glucose meters, insulin infusion pumps, blood pressure monitors, and automatic drug injectors) have been designed for a broad user population—including people who do not have medical training. This broadening of user populations has forced medical device companies to redefine their way of thinking about violations. Actions that previously might have been called violations are to be classified as "foreseeable human errors," which may have to be considered in design or instructions.

Human processing categories: perception, cognition, and action. Another aid for identifying use errors is to consider processing stages in human behavior; namely, perception, cognition, and action (PCA). We will not delve into the large body of psychological research on PCA but use it as a framework for identifying failures (errors) in one of the following categories.

- *Perception*: the sensory input and processing used during performance of a task.
- *Cognition*: the mental processing—including the use of short- and long-term memory—required to perform a task.
- *Action*: the action (or output) taken by the user.

Here are the steps for identifying errors based on PCA.

1. For each task and subtask, consider which PCA elements are required to perform the task. Examples of how tasks could be broken into PCA components are shown in the left column of Table 3.3.

Table 3.3. Examples of a Task Statement Decomposed into PCA Subtasks

Task statement: *The user inserts the pain medication cartridge into the infusion pump and activates the locking lever to seat the cartridge.*

PCA Subtasks	Possible Errors
Perception (P)	
• User reads the cartridge identification (name and concentration).	• User does not see identification label. • User incorrectly reads the identification. • User incorrectly reads concentration. • User fails to read concentration.
• User views cartridge to determine orientation. • User sees/locates the cartridge slot. • User sees the locking lever.	• User does not see orientation cues. • User cannot see/has difficulty finding cartridge slot. • User has difficulty seeing the locking lever.
Cognition (C)	
• User mentally matches the name and concentration of the medication.	• User misinterprets the cartridge name and/ or concentration. • User transposes numbers for concentration. • User mistakes another drug name for current Rx (e.g., look-alike, sound-alike drug names).
• User remembers/determines proper orientation of cartridge for insertion.	• User misinterprets orientation cues.
• User remembers/determines which way the locking lever is activated to close.	• User misinterprets cues for locking.
• User remembers to close the locking lever.	• User forgets to close lever.
Action (A)	
• User picks up medication cartridge.	• User picks up the wrong medication cartridge. • User drops cartridge.
• User inserts cartridge into slot.	• User inserts cartridge with too little force. • User inserts cartridge too forcefully. • User inserts cartridge upside down. • User inserts cartridge backwards.
• User activates locking lever.	• User does not to activate the locking lever. • User attempts to push lever, but it is not fully seated.

Note: Possible use errors are characterized for each PCA subtask.

2. For each PCA component identified, brainstorm with your team about how the component could fail. For perception, the description should be related to the failure to perceive a sensory input. For cognition, the failure should be related to failure to correctly process a sensory input or to a user memory failure. Action will be related to, for example, a user's failure to touch a button or voice a command. Examples for potential errors/faults are shown in the right-hand column of Table 3.3.

Step 4: Identify Potential Effects of Each Use Error/Failure Mode

In this step, the team will analyze and document the potential effects or harm resulting from the failure mode if it occurs. This step is needed for establishing risk ratings, which follows. Each effect can be thought of as an if-then process ("if [specified error] occurs, then [specified harm] could be the result").

Many devices, such as motorized hospital beds, infusion pumps, surgical robots, imaging systems, and radiation therapy devices, can cause direct harm to the patient or user if used incorrectly. Other devices potentially can be the source of indirect harm. For example, an in vitro diagnostic blood glucose test that fails to accurately measure glucose levels does not directly harm a patient. However, the patient may be harmed indirectly if they receive inappropriate treatment due to the incorrect test result.

For most medical devices, the harm could have implications for the patient and/or the user, ranging from minor to severe injury or even death, depending on the nature of the device. If multiple harms are involved, the convention is to consider the reasonable worst-case harm scenario.

Step 5: Assign Severity Ratings for the Harm

A severity rating is a qualitative (descriptive) or numeric rating of the seriousness of the effects of the harm caused by a fault (if it occurs). With medical devices, the highest severity ratings are typically reserved for faults that have severe consequences for the patient or user, usually involving severe injury or death. You would assign lower ratings to noninjury or minor effects, such as customer inconvenience or annoyance, or minor reversible injuries, such as a scrape or pinch. For many medical devices, we advise that ratings of severity be provided or approved by your medical affairs group or equivalent.

Depending on the method used, severity can be assigned a numeric value or a qualitative rating. Quantitative ratings are typically specified with ranges of 1–5 or 1–10, with 1 being the lowest severity and 5 (or 10) being the highest. Table 3.4 shows an example of numeric ratings with a range of 1–5 with accompanying qualitative descriptors.

Qualitative severity ratings provide similar gradations, which typically include up to five severity levels. In the example shown in Table 3.5, three levels of severity—minimal, moderate, and major—include descriptions for each level. The number of levels is up to the team (or is often specified by company procedures); however, it is extremely difficult to specify more than five levels that are discriminable and memorable.

Step 6: Estimate Occurrence (Probability) of Use Error Leading to Harm

Occurrence ratings are estimates of the probability of occurrence (or the predicted frequency) of a fault that can lead to harm. It is best to base occurrence ratings on existing data, such as customer complaint data, telephone support center call data, and usability test results. When such data are not available, occurrence ratings will be estimated by the collective judgment of the FMEA team.

Table 3.4. Example of Numeric Severity Ratings with Definitions and Qualitative Labels ("Severity Category")

Severity Category	Severity Rating	Consequences to Patients, Users, or Environment
Catastrophic	5	May cause death, total loss of operation, or severe impact on the environment that causes death or total loss of operation.
Critical	4	May cause permanent injury, permanent occupational illness, major and recoverable damage to operation, or major and recoverable impact on the environment.
Significant	3	May cause recoverable injury, recoverable occupational illness, major and recoverable damage to operation, or major and recoverable impact on the environment.
Marginal	2	May cause minor injury, minor occupational illness, or minor impact on operation or the environment.
Negligible	1	Will not result in significant injury, occupational illness, or a significant impact on the environment. Negligible effect on operation.

Table 3.5. Example of Qualitative Severity Ratings

Severity Rating	Consequences
Major	The hazard could directly result in death or serious injury of the patient or operator, or indirectly affect the patient such that delayed or incorrect information could result in death or serious injury to the patient.
Moderate	The hazard could directly result in moderate injury to the patient or operator, or indirectly affect the patient such that delayed or incorrect information could result in moderate injury to the patient.
Minimal	The hazard is not expected to result in negative medical consequences or any complication.

Table 3.6. Example of Numeric Ratings for Probability of Occurrence with Qualitative Descriptors

Frequency Category	Numeric Rating	Frequency of Occurrence
Extremely likely	5	Very high probability of occurrence
Likely	4	High probability of occurrence
Possible	3	Moderate probability of occurrence
Unlikely	2	Low probability of occurrence
Extremely unlikely	1	Very low or remote probability of occurrence

As with severity ratings, occurrence ratings can be assigned a numeric value, typically 1–5 or 1–10, with 1 being the lowest frequency of occurrence and 5 (or 10) being the highest. Table 3.6 shows a representative example of a numeric occurrence rating scale along with accompanying descriptors for each level.

Table 3.7. Example of Qualitative Ratings for Probability of Occurrence in FMEA

Probability of Occurrence Rating	Description
Probable	Likely to occur regularly or many times during the life of the product under specified operating conditions.
Occasional	Likely to occur infrequently or several times during the life of the product under specified operating conditions.
Rare	Will rarely occur or is very unlikely to occur during the life of the product under specified operating conditions.
Improbable	Not expected to occur under specified operating conditions.

Probability ratings can also be designated using qualitative ratings. Table 3.7 provides an example of qualitative probability ratings with four occurrence levels ranging from lowest to highest probability: improbable, rare, occasional, and probable. The number of levels is up to the team; however, most qualitative ratings rarely exceed five levels.

When estimating the probability of occurrence of a device use error leading to harm, over what period should the estimate be made?

The estimate should be based on use during the lifetime of the product. If data are available on a monthly or annual basis, the data should be extrapolated to the anticipated duration of the product life.

Step 7: Assign a Risk Index

In risk analysis terms, risk is defined by the combination of the severity of the hazard and its probability of occurrence. When using numeric values, a risk index or risk level is calculated by multiplying the severity rating (in Step 5) by the occurrence rating (in Step 6). The range of values in 5-point scales for severity and occurrence can range from 1 (1 × 1) to 25 (5 × 5); and for a 10-point scale, the values can range from 1 to 100.

Risk = Severity × Occurrence

The risk index for qualitative ratings is also determined by combining ratings for occurrence and severity. Table 1.2 (page 9) illustrates how risk indices could be defined using three levels of severity (major, moderate, and minimal) and four levels of occurrence (probable, occasional, rare, and improbable). Each combination of occurrence and severity yields a qualitative risk index rating: high, medium, and low. For example, an event that has an occurrence rating of probable with a severity of major results in a high risk. A rare event with moderate severity results in a low risk.

In recent years, regulators such as the FDA have been concerned that some high-severity harms are not always given serious consideration for mitigation when rated with low probability ratings. Their main concern is that a failure mode that has potentially severe consequences could be overlooked if probability ratings were (intentionally or unintentionally) underestimated. As a consequence, some manufacturers have mandated that the risk level for a harm with high severity be rated moderate or high *regardless of the rated probability*. Similarly, another common conservative practice is to assign a default probability equal to 1.00 (100% probability) or high probability (if ratings are qualitative).

We often lack data to estimate probability of occurrence of use errors. Why bother estimating?

With human factors applications, we seldom have quantitative data that enable us to predict use errors with the same precision as component failure and system reliability predictions made by systems engineers (e.g., failure rates in parts per million). Although usability tests can provide statistical data regarding human-machine interaction, the small sample sizes typically used in experiments limit our ability to predict probability of success with high levels of precision. Consequently, we are left to rely on expert judgment for estimating failure probability. Some believe that analyses that rely on expert judgments instead of data are not legitimate and should not be done.

Engineers also have to estimate probability. Although reliability and system engineers have long used component and subsystem failure test data to predict failure rates, the notion that objective data are always available and that probability estimates are never relied on by the system designers is simply incorrect. With systems in early development, systems that are unique, or those that use components lacking statistical test data, there are often insufficient data to support direct probability estimation. In such cases, engineers have long had to estimate failure probabilities.

Someone will make a judgment regarding acceptance of risk. Before a product is released, project managers must assess whether a device or system is ready to be launched. At various times during development, the use error team may be asked to give judgments regarding specific risks. If the team is unable or unwilling to make such judgments, someone else will.

The following are examples of questions that a use error team might be asked to address while having to give justifications for the answer.

- Is it ok if we release the product and implement the mitigation in the next version of the software?
- Which of the two (or more) design mitigations provides greater risk reduction?
- Will instructions and training reduce the risk to an acceptable level?
- Does applying two mitigations reduce risk more than either mitigation alone?
- Now that the mitigation has been implemented, have we reached an acceptable level of risk?

Using severity only. With the lack of probability data, some argue that the risk of a use error should be determined solely on severity (or task criticality) and that probability should be ignored. Although this approach can be useful in initially selecting mitigation targets, not considering probability raises some problematic issues, such as these.

- When risk is estimated after applying mitigations, severity is usually not affected. If probability of occurrence is ignored, how do we show that risk is lowered?

- If multiple mitigations are being considered for a given use error, how do we assess the effectiveness of the mitigations if not by reducing probability of occurrence?
- Without estimates of probability, how do we assess that a given mitigation is better than none? And how do we assess whether two (redundant design) mitigations are better than one?

As discussed in Chapters 1, 6, and 7, the FDA has recommended an alternative to uFMEA, use-related risk analysis (URRA). The method avoids the use of probability estimates for initial risk by first identifying critical tasks, which, if performed incorrectly, can affect safe operation. Although the method provides a means to address critical use error risks, it fails to make clear how mitigations and residual risk can be resolved without assessing the likelihood of error. We believe that estimates of probability are necessary.

Step 8: Prioritize the Failure Modes (Use Errors) by Risk Level

For complex systems, it is neither feasible nor practical to eliminate all possible risks in the system. The designation of risk indices enables risks to be prioritized so that those with high severity and probability can be discriminated from risks with low severity and probability, on the assumption that some risks may be so low as to not justify devoting resources to their mitigation.

Failure modes are sorted according to their risk index (either quantitative or qualitative), from the highest to lowest. The team or company should prespecify the criteria that they will use to decide a boundary (or cut-off) above which the application of mitigations/modes of control must be applied in order to reduce the risk level. In the absence of such guidelines, you will need to establish ground rules for deciding. It is advisable to standardize decision criteria within the device development group or at a higher organizational level. Similar decision criteria could be established by means of numeric categories when using numeric indices.

Prioritization may include special procedural rules that are predetermined by company, division, or work group policies. For example, a manufacturer could require that failure modes with high severity ratings be automatically designated as high risk, regardless of probability of occurrence. Such rules could guard against inadvertent, inaccurate, or unreliable underestimation of the probability of occurrence. In another example, a company procedure could dictate that failure modes with high risk levels automatically require the use of design mitigations instead of instructional mitigations. Such rules could provide a procedural safeguard against assigning a less reliable mode of control (see the next section) to a failure mode with substantial risk.

Step 9: List the Method of Control (Mitigations) for Each Failure Mode/Use Error

As stated earlier, during this phase, your team will brainstorm mitigations that are designed to reduce probability and/or severity. Attention should be given first to failure modes that are rated higher in risk.

Mitigations are modifications to the design of the user interface (hardware, software, instructional materials, or training). Such mitigations can be thought of as filters of use errors. Some design mitigations could be 100% effective in preventing certain types of error or reducing their effect, but most are not. For each failure mode, the team's challenge is to identify mitigations that will have the largest filtering effect without disproportionately decreasing usability or increasing costs or development time. The use of additional redundant mitigations should be considered when a single mitigation is not totally effective. Also, because some mitigations can have their own failure modes, mitigations may need their own mitigations. This point will be illustrated in the example case studies in Chapters 5 and 6.

When use error risks are thought to be high or uncertain, formative usability tests can be an essential tool in determining the effectiveness of mitigations. In such tests, mock-ups of hardware, software, or instructional materials are presented to users in a scenario that simulates the risk scenario. The results from a study that includes a representative sample of users can be used to determine if the risk has been reduced or if further mitigations are needed.

Instructional materials and warnings as mitigations for use errors. As discussed in Chapter 1, instructional information (manuals, reference guides, labels, etc.) that include warnings, cautions, and alerts are often proposed as a means to reduce the risk associated with use errors. The challenge with instructional materials and warnings is that a proportion of users do not read, pay attention to, understand, remember, or comply with instructions. That is why instructional materials are considered to be a less effective way of reducing the probability of use errors.

In-person training is often proposed as a means to reduce use errors. One challenge with such training is that manufacturers typically provide training to a limited number of key operators for a device, who are then tasked with training other users through in-service training sessions. Even if the training level is universal across all users, training itself remains an imperfect method for eliminating use errors, especially in systems that are used infrequently or when long periods elapse between training and actual use.

As with design-related modes of control, when instructional materials and training are cited as the means to mitigate use errors, the FDA and other regulatory agencies require that the effectiveness of instructional modes of control be demonstrated through testing (i.e., validated) with target users.

Step 10: Determine If New Hazards Have Been Introduced or If Estimated Risks for Other Hazards Have Been Affected

During brainstorming, your team is likely to list multiple ways to mitigate a given failure mode, some of which will be better than others for reducing risk. While intending to reduce the risk for a particular hazard, it is possible that the mitigation can increase risk in other areas. This "regression effect" can happen in one of two ways: the mitigation introduces an unanticipated new hazard, or the mitigation affects the probability and/or severity of other hazardous situations (ISO, 2019). To guard against these possibilities, ISO 14971 suggests that each mitigation be analyzed for such possibilities before implementation.

Usability tests should be conducted to determine if any unintended effects exist. Results should be fed back to risk management and design teams.

Step 11: Assign Effectiveness Ratings of Mitigations on Risk Level

In this step, your team will revise the estimates of probability of occurrence of harm and/or the severity for each failure mode with the previously specified mitigations in place. For a quantitative risk index, the risk level is recomputed based on the revised (mitigated) probability of occurrence and/or severity. For qualitative analyses, the risk index will be updated based on the revised qualitative occurrence and severity ratings. Both will result in a new risk level.

Although it is tempting to assume that the mitigations proposed will be totally effective in reducing the risk, you should consider the following questions:

- Will the mitigation be effective enough to cause a (qualitative or quantitative) rating change in occurrence?
- What could happen that would prevent the mitigation from being effective?
- Does the mitigation affect the severity of the harm?

As always, usability testing should be employed to assess doubts about effectiveness.

Does the mitigation affect severity or occurrence? Although mitigations can theoretically affect probability of occurrence, severity, or both, in our experience, mitigations most often affect the probability of occurrence but not severity.

In some situations, the severity of a hazard is reduced. For example, suppose a device that is designed for use near water is powered by normal line voltage (e.g., 110VAC or 220VAC). Typical design mitigations such as isolation (insulation), proper grounding, and ground-fault circuit interruption (GFCI) circuitry are mitigations that serve to reduce the probability of electrocution to a low level by preventing exposure to high voltage. However, exposure of the user to high voltage that is present in the device (improbable though it might be) could lead to severe injury or death—an event with a high severity rating. Suppose the device were redesigned to operate solely on a low-voltage battery and had no internal high-voltage circuits. Because exposure to low voltage is unlikely to cause electrocution, the severity rating would be low or zero. If previous isolation measures are maintained, the combination of low occurrence and low severity would result in a low risk index.

Directly estimate the effect of the mitigation on risk. Another way to assess the effect of mitigations skips the separate postmitigation rating of probability of occurrence and severity. Instead, the method requires raters to determine if the risk level either remains the same as it was prior to the mitigation or is reduced. If reduced, to what level? For example, in an FMEA in which risk is rated as high, medium, or low, the effectiveness rating could be defined by the following choices:

- does not change (i.e., the planned mitigation is not effective)
- reduces (risk) to medium
- reduces (risk) to low.

Step 12: Assess Whether or Not Residual Risk Levels Are Acceptable

Here your team will determine if the residual risk for each failure mode has been reduced to an acceptable level. Each organization should have predetermined decision rules regarding acceptance levels. For example, in Table 3.8, we propose three levels of residual risk and their acceptability.

Table 3.8. Residual Risk and Acceptance Levels

Residual Risk	Acceptability
Low	Acceptable. The failure presents low or no risk to patient or user.
Medium	Acceptable with justification.
High	Not acceptable. Presents a significant safety risk to patient and/or user.

An item that has low residual risk is deemed acceptable, requiring no further action. On the opposite end of the spectrum, an item with a high residual risk rating is deemed not acceptable. Typically, regulatory and company guidelines will mandate that a device cannot be released for manufacture with failure modes having high residual risk. The failure mode with high residual risk will require further mitigations to reduce the risk to an acceptable level. If further mitigation is not possible or deemed not cost-effective, the product may be declared unsafe and therefore nonviable. Such a declaration could ultimately constitute the end of the project.

The level between the two extremes, medium, is considered "acceptable with justification." This rating signifies that the residual risk may not be further reducible or has reached the level as low as reasonably practicable (ALARP), as described in Chapter 1. In such cases, justification must be presented in the form of a benefit-to-risk analysis describing why the benefits of the device outweigh the possible harm resulting from the failure mode. It should not be merely justification for why the risk cannot be further reduced. Examples of the benefit–risk trade-off are illustrated in Chapter 1.

Step 13: Repeat Steps 9–12 Until Risks Are at Acceptable Levels

Iterate until each residual risk is at or below the acceptance criteria.

FMEA Variations

FMEAs can take many forms. Here we discuss some common variations in FMEA presentations.

Can uFMEA be combined with design FMEA (dFMEA)?

Yes. The other question that is often asked is, "Must the uFMEA and the design FMEA be separate documents?" Although you should check with your regulatory agency before committing formats, there are advantages for either approach.

Advantages of an integrated document include the following.

- Interaction of the different teams through a single document could provide mutual insights into potential failure modes and their modes of control that separate documents could not.
- Inconsistencies or conflicts between the documents would be easier to discover and resolve.
- Integrating two documents into a single document could uncover differences and inconsistencies that may not be detected otherwise. For example, some hazards and harms have different wording; inconsistent criteria are used for ratings of occurrence and severity; and inconsistent rules are used to determine the risk level cut-off criteria for application of modes of control.

Note that for audits, if dFMEAs and uFMEAs are merged, it may be useful to assign a column in the FMEA to designate whether the failure mode is a design or use issue. If a uFMEA or dFMEA is requested during an audit, the human factors items can be separated from the dFMEAs by sorting or filtering the worksheet for separate review.

Advantages of separate documents. A team performing uFMEA will often develop an analysis document that differs from the document developed by the team performing the dFMEA. Differences in schedules or regulatory needs could justify the continued use of separate documents. Even so, it's a good idea to compare documents for reasons that include finding inconsistencies listed earlier, discovering failure modes that were overlooked, eliminating redundancies (same items that exist in both documents), and determining if the same mitigations can be used.

Numeric Versus Descriptive (Qualitative) Ratings

Numeric ratings for risk (quantitative or semiquantitative) such as RPN (which will be discussed later) have been in use for decades. It is commonly believed that numeric indexes make estimates using them more accurate or scientific. However, when dealing with uFMEAs (or other FMEAs lacking data)—whether using numeric or qualitative ratings—occurrence ratings for use errors will almost certainly involve categorical (qualitative) ratings rather than precise numerical values for probability. Numeric values for severity also are accompanied by categorical descriptions. Consequently, it makes little practical difference whether numeric or descriptive ratings are used; that is a matter of team or company standards or preference. We don't have a preference. Table 3.9 compares two examples of risk components for qualitative and quantitative entries.

Occurrence ratings are often the most challenging for teams to establish. Stamatis (1995) offers examples of quantitative benchmarks for machine failures in terms of expected frequencies (probabilities), in which occurrence "rankings" are rated from 1 to 10 with corresponding probabilities of 1 in 10,000 (for rank 1) to 1 in 10 (for rank 10). These statistically derived categories are based on the number of outliers expected at specified standard deviations from the mean (showing 1 in 10,000 is based on $\bar{X} \pm 3\ \sigma$). As stated earlier, although it is possible to estimate failure probabilities when dealing with electrical or mechanical components, for which extensive test data are typically available, estimating failure probabilities for human error is an entirely different matter.

The FDA has rejected manufacturers' premarket product submissions that use low-confidence probability estimates to inappropriately dismiss further analysis of some use errors that can lead to death or serious harm. For this reason, as mentioned in Chapter 1,

Table 3.9. Comparison of Example Qualitative and Quantitative FMEA Risk Components

Method	Risk Severity	Fault Probability	Risk Level	Mitigation Effectiveness	Outcome (Residual Risk)
Qualitative	Major Moderate Minimal	Probable Occasional Rare Improbable	High Medium Low	No change Lower Eliminate	Unacceptable Acceptable w/justification Acceptable
Quantitative	5 4 3 2 1	5 4 3 2 1	1–25	1 2 3 4 5	> 45 Unacceptable 9 < 45 Acceptable w/review 1 < 9 Acceptable

the FDA has proposed use of the URRA method, which eliminates probability estimates altogether and focuses exclusively on severity of harm. See Chapter 6 for an example of URRA and Chapter 7 for further discussion.

Number of Categories (or Intervals) for Severity and Occurrence

With use of numeric ratings, the ratings for severity (S), occurrence (O), and detectability (D) are multiplied to form a "risk priority number" (RPN). A risk index or risk level that we discuss in this book (that excludes detectability for reasons described later in this chapter) is calculated by multiplying severity of harm (S, typically 1–5 or 1–10) by occurrence of harm (O, also typically 1–5 or 1–10), thus yielding risk indices in the ranges of 1–25 or 1–100. (Note that this value technically cannot be referred to as RPN because it does not include detection as a factor.) Qualitative ratings for occurrence and severity typically employ up to five rating levels for each.

A common notion is that the larger the number of gradations in a rating, the more precise or accurate it is. If that is the case, what would be the problem with increasing the range of ratings to 1–100 or higher? Extensive psychological literature on the topic of psychophysics has shown that when people are required to make absolute judgments of a physical stimulus such as color or pure auditory tones, the number of reliable judgments they can make along the dimension are surprisingly small—ranging from 5 to 9 or 7 ± 2, as stated in Sanders and McCormick (1993). In other words, despite the fact that there are many thousands of discriminable colors in the visual spectrum, humans can reliably identify only about 5 to 9 of them. The relatively small number is theorized to be related to limitations in human memory.

Because the task of estimating levels of severity and occurrence is much more complex and likely more variable than judging colors or pure tones, we contend that the number of categories for rating severity or probability of occurrence—whether qualitative or quantitative—is similarly limited. Using a large range of ratings, such as 1–100 or higher, implies a (false) level of precision or accuracy that cannot be justified. Furthermore, in our experience, using a large number of categories will substantially increase the team's time and effort to rate, discuss, and reach consensus on the resultant outcomes without yielding incremental benefit. We recommend about 5 levels and certainly no more than 10.

Scaling

Despite the fact that numeric ratings of severity and occurrence typically use intervals of 1–5 or 1–10, we cannot assume that the differences between consecutive numbers represent intervals with equal differences between successive values. They merely represent the rank-order of these categories. Therefore, a severity rating of 4 is not necessarily twice that of a rating of 2, nor is a probability rating of 1 half as likely as a rating of 2.

When computing risk indexes (or RPN), multiplying severity by occurrence (and by detection for RPN), the resultant values for risk index should not be considered precise calculations. Rather, consider them as an ordinal basis for rank ordering. Regarding RPN, Stamatis (1995) states that "[the] value by itself should be used only to rank order [the] . . . concerns of the system, design, product, process and service. All RPNs have no other value or meaning" (p. 35).

Detectability

As noted earlier, in addition to ratings for severity and occurrence, the calculation of RPN includes a third rating: detectability. This rating is used, particularly in manufacturing process settings, to characterize the ability of the process or user to detect and prevent a problem or fault before it occurs. In contrast to severity and occurrence ratings, the numeric rating for detectability is defined in reverse order, where high detectability is given a low numeric value (e.g., 1) and the lowest detectability is given a high number (e.g., 10). So, if detectability is high, the resultant RPN value, defined by RPN = Severity × Occurrence × Detectability, will remain low. If detectability is low (with a high numeric score), RPN increases. We and others offer the following reasons why detectability may not be appropriate for uFMEAs.

First, as pointed out by Schmidt (2004), detection of a hazard during device use may not ensure that harm will be avoided. He poses these three questions, which delineate conditions that could determine if detectability would serve to prevent harm:

1. Is there enough time to react after detection?
2. Is information provided to the user to indicate specific actions for avoiding the harm?
3. Will the user have the presence of mind to remember what is done and take action?

Second, in situations when a user can detect a problem and prevent harm, we contend that this should be factored into the probability of occurrence of the use error itself. If detectability is enabled by the user interface in a way that will reduce the overall probability of occurrence (or the severity), that constitutes a mode of control and therefore should be reflected by a reduction in the probability of occurrence (or, where appropriate, severity).

Also, if detection is treated as an independent numeric factor of the RPN, its inclusion could artificially inflate the RPN value even when detection is rated low (say, 2 or 3).

Mitigation Effectiveness

As the name implies, mitigation effectiveness ratings are used by some to characterize how effective a specific mitigation is in reducing the risk. As with detectability, mitigation effectiveness ratings are used as a third rating (e.g., Severity × Occurrence × Mitigation Effectiveness). As with detectability, numeric ratings are defined in reverse order, where high effectiveness is given a low numeric value and low effectiveness is given a high value. If mitigation effectiveness is high (with a low numeric score), the overall risk number—defined by Severity × Occurrence × Mitigation Effectiveness—tends to remain low or the same. If mitigation effectiveness is low (high numeric score), the overall risk number increases.

There are at least two caveats when using mitigation effectiveness. First, if mitigation effectiveness ratings are used, postmitigation ratings of severity and occurrence should not (also) be used to reflect the effects of mitigation. Doing so could artificially bias the resultant risk outcome. Second, the reverse numeric scheme typically allows a rating of 1 when a mitigation is maximally effective. If the overall risk index is unacceptably high, the risk mitigation rating precludes reducing the overall risk number to an acceptable level, unless a compensating method (such as reducing the rating below 1) is devised.

Advantages and Disadvantages of FMEA

FMEA is a straightforward method for documenting potential failures in terms of risk, enabling explicit documentation of the modes of control or mitigations for each failure mode. For these reasons, FMEA has apparently become the most commonly used method of documenting risk management.

Because of its bottom-up nature, whereby faults in the FMEA are dealt with one item (failure mode) at a time, it is often difficult to characterize and assess how a given fault or

Table 3.10. Advantages and Disadvantages of FMEA

Advantages	Disadvantages
1. Risk index enables prioritization of failure modes. 2. Explicitly documents modes of control/mitigation. 3. Format is useful for tracking action items. 4. Straightforward construction is possible using computer-based software tools: a. Spreadsheets/word-processing tables b. Database tools (DBMS) c. Specialized FMEA tools 5. Does not require complex computation.	1. Difficult to assess combination of events and complex interactions. 2. Large documents can be difficult to manage to minimize inconsistencies and redundant items. 3. Severity and occurrence ratings are often difficult for individuals or teams to estimate. Lack of benchmarks can make ratings difficult to defend. 4. FMEA deals with one failure mode at a time—does not easily deal with combinatorial effect of events. • Could miss hazards that occur only with multiple combinatorial fault conditions. • Multiple fault conditions may have to be combined into one failure mode description (scenario).

use error can lead to the ultimate undesired event. In situations in which multiple failures must occur to create a hazardous situation, the characterization of the particular failure mode can misrepresent the overall probability of failure. In such situations, fault tree analysis (FTA) is a good complementary method for identifying what combination of events must occur for a harm to occur and the probability of its happening. Some risk management practitioners espouse the use of an FTA for every input to an FMEA when a combination of multiple failures might occur, whereas others limit use of FTAs to chosen complex or risky scenarios. Table 3.10 summarizes advantages and disadvantages of using FMEA.

4 Fault Tree Analysis

Fault tree analysis, like FMEA, is a tool for analyzing and predicting failure. Unlike FMEA, which starts with individual faults and predicts effects on system operation and safety in a bottom-up approach, FTA is a deductive, top-down method that starts with an assumed undesired event and identifies faults that cause the event. Also, unlike FMEA, fault trees are depicted graphically.

FTA is a rigorous method for deducing root cause(s) of an undesired event or hazard and to determine system or subsystem reliability and safety. The main benefits and uses for fault trees are the following.

- Identifies the combination of events and conditions that lead to the undesired event/hazard.
- Can be used to compute the probability of an undesired event/hazard.
- Can be used to compute system and subsystem reliability and safety.
- Can be used to estimate the relative impact of use errors.
- Can be used to estimate the relative impact of faults and mitigations on the probability of an undesired event.
- Can be used to compare alternative designs.
- Illustrates, through diagrams, vulnerabilities to faults and use errors.
- Can be used, through review of diagrams, for sensitivity analysis of which event combinations have more impact on fault probabilities.

FTA has been used extensively in aerospace, nuclear power, military, and petrochemical applications in which consequences of system or human failure can have catastrophic consequences. In recent years, fault trees have also been used in pharmaceutical and medical applications.

For human factors applications, FTA can be an extremely useful tool for visualizing the contributing effects of human error (use error), device faults on overall system operation, as well as environmental events. A unique advantage of FTAs over other risk analysis methods is that by assigning probability estimates to individual faults, including use errors, you can use combinatorial probability rules to calculate estimates of failure probability and the effects of modes of control to reduce those probabilities.

The following section describes basic steps in developing fault trees. In the case study in Chapter 5, we provide an FTA for a hypothetical automatic external defibrillator (AED). We suggest that you refer to the FTA literature for more detailed information on fundamentals of this analysis method. Comprehensive descriptions of fault tree analysis can be found in handbooks by the U.S. Nuclear Regulatory Commission (1981) and NASA (2002).

Basic Elements of a Fault Tree

A fault tree starts with a single undesired event, represented by a rectangle at the top of an inverted tree containing the top-level event (undesired fault event), with contributory events or conditions that can lead to the undesired event branching downward level by level. Most events will be stated as faults or failures. However, normal (nonfault) conditions can also be included. Each event is connected to lower "child" branches that identify the causes for the "parent" event. The relationship between parent and child events is represented by logical (Boolean) symbols or "gates," as shown in Table 4.1.

Table 4.1. Fault Tree Symbols and Use

 Basic event	A basic component failure or use error.	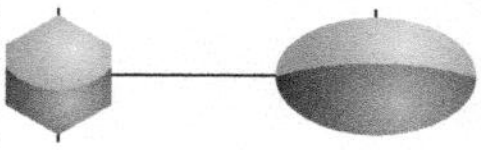 Inhibit gate	A certain condition of the system must exist before one failure produces another. The inhibit condition may be either normal to the system or the result of failure.
 Undeveloped event	A component or use error that has not been fully developed due to the lack of information or significance.	 Exclusive OR gate	Output occurs if any input occurs; specified inputs are mutually exclusive.
 House event	A normally occurring, nonfailure event in the system.	 NOR gate	Output occurs when all the input events are absent.
 OR gate	Output occurs if any of the input events occurs.	 NOT gate	Output occurs when the input event does not occur.
 AND gate	Output occurs if all of the inputs occur.	 NAND gate	Output occurs when at least one of the input events is absent.
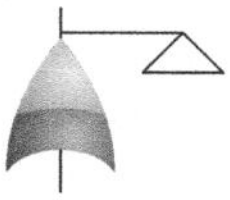 Transfer gate	Symbol used to link elements in a fault tree with other pages or other segments of the tree.	 Priority AND gate	Output occurs when all inputs occur in the sequence specified.
 Voting gate	Output occurs if a specified number of events occurs. The input events need not occur simultaneously.		

The most commonly used event symbols shown in the left half of the table are basic, undeveloped, or "house" events. A basic event is an event (fault) that cannot be further decomposed into constituent failures. An undeveloped event is one that may have more constituent failures but currently lacks detailed information. Undeveloped event symbols are usually used for events that do not have a major effect on the system and may be used as a placeholder for subsequent analysis if necessary. A house event is one that does not constitute a fault

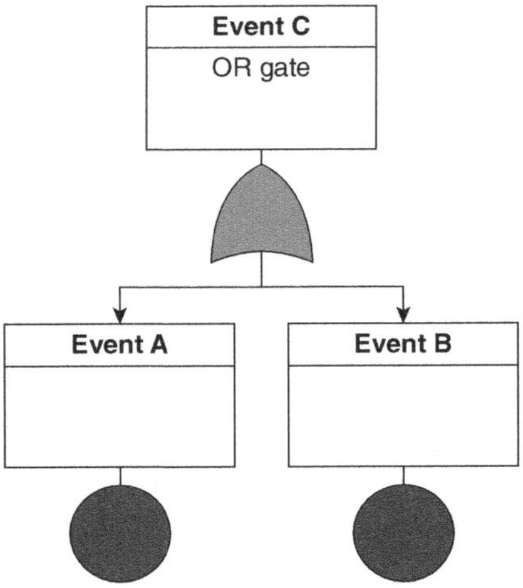

Figure 4.1. OR gate with input events A and B and output event C.

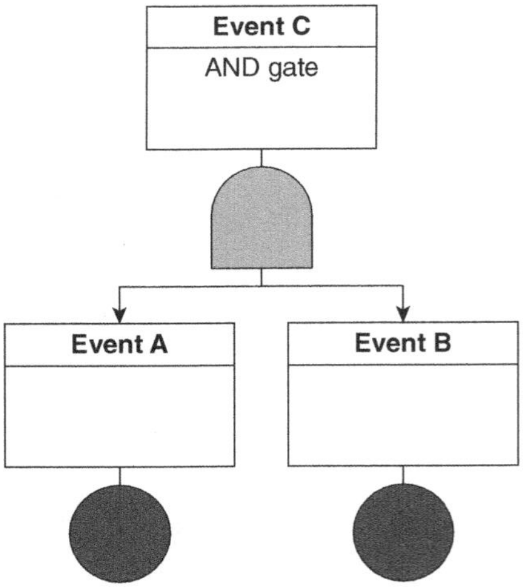

Figure 4.2. AND gate with inputs A and B and output event C.

event but is a normally expected event in the system. House events, sometimes called a "trigger" or "normal" event, are used to represent situations when a normally occurring system event can trigger a failure when combined with other fault conditions. An example is the activation of a switch that results in an arc that triggers an explosion due to the presence of combustible gas in an enclosed space.

The event (in the rectangular box) above each gate is the "output" event, and the items connected to the bottom of the gate are the "input" events. While a gate can have any number of input events, it can have only one output event. The gates shown in Table 4.1 can be used depending on which logical input conditions cause the output to occur.

The most commonly used gates are the "OR" gate and the "AND" gate. The OR gate, shown in Figure 4.1, is depicted with two inputs, A and B. The output of the gate, event C, occurs if either A occurs, if B occurs, or if both A and B occur. The AND gate shown in Figure 4.2 also has two inputs, events A and B. However, the AND gate output, event C, occurs only if both events A and B occur.

You may need to use other gates shown in Table 4.1, but we recommend using them judiciously; that is, only when the device logic and operation require them. The use of some gates can cause confusion when discussing various scenarios that include normal and inverse logic, especially for those who have had limited exposure to digital logic. For example, a NOT gate is one that is used to "invert" the output of an event or gate. So if it is attached to an input event, that means the event triggers (true) only if the event does not occur. If the event occurs, there is no output. If it is mixed in with normal (noninverted) logic, it is easy to see how tracing the events through a fault tree could cause confusion.

Fault Tree Development Tools

Fault trees can be developed using general-purpose drawing programs that are available for personal computers, such as Visio® and Smartdraw®. These tools provide symbol libraries and templates for FTAs that include event and Boolean symbols that enable relatively rapid drawing of fault trees with familiar drag-and-drop operations.

In recent years, specialized risk analysis software programs have been developed specifically for creating and editing FTAs (as well as FMEAs). In addition to offering standard templates and symbol libraries, FTA tools have capabilities that are not available in drawing programs, such as the ability to automatically calculate branch and top-level probabilities and to perform Monte Carlo simulations to assess the statistical variability of systems. Such tools make FTAs' strengths much more accessible and less labor-intensive than manual methods. Most of the fault trees shown in this chapter were created (in color but shown in black and white) with Relyence Fault Tree Analysis by Relyence Corporation.

Basic Steps in Conducting an FTA

The following outline shows the steps for fault tree development, starting with the top-level event and then decomposing events into constituent causes until reaching the bottom of the tree.

Step 1: Identify the Undesired Event To Be Analyzed (Top-Level Hazard)

Your team may decide to develop FTAs for all hazards in the system or only for selected hazards.

Step 2: Build the Fault Tree

After you have determined the top-level event, building the fault tree involves identifying its causes (fault conditions) and connecting them using the appropriate gates described earlier. Cause can include

- events that may lead directly to harm (single-point failure) or cause another fault without other events occurring,
- events that may be faults (failures),
- normal (nonfault) system events,
- events that must happen in conjunction with other events to cause failure, and
- events that must happen in sequence to cause a failure.

Failure modes and failure mechanisms. Earlier we described the structure of FTAs as having a series of parent-child relationships. Another way to think of FTAs is in terms of "failure modes" and "failure mechanisms." For a given event, failure modes identify the components of concern for that event. Failure mechanisms are events that explain how a particular failure mode can occur. Stated another way, failure mechanisms are the means by which a failure mode occurs (NASA, 2002).

After determining the top-level event, you will identify its failure modes and then the failure mechanisms for each failure mode. For the next level, you will regard each mechanism as a failure mode and identify the failure mechanisms for it. As you proceed down the tree, you will repeat this alternating focus between failure mode and failure mechanism until reaching the bottom of the tree.

"Small steps." When identifying the causal events for each fault, you will be determining the most closely related event, with each level taking a "small step" (the most immediate cause) rather than one that jumps directly to a basic event. Small steps will ensure that all the primary causes and their relationships are identified.

Figure 4.3 presents an example FTA for a scenario in which a light fails to turn on when the switch is activated (top-level event). The events below the top-level event are

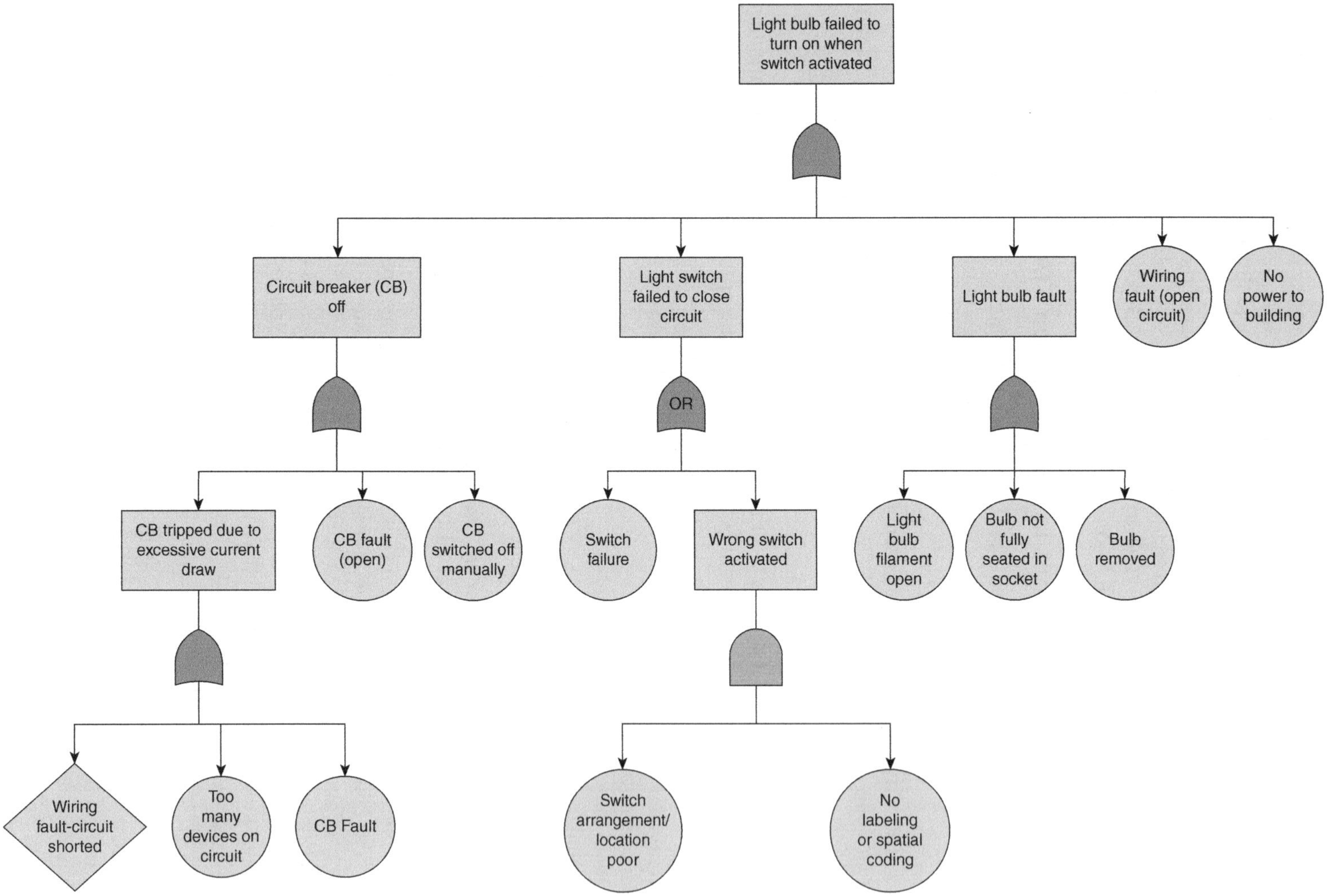

Figure 4.3. Fault tree for "Light bulb failed to turn on when switch activated."

its causes: (1) no power to the building, (2) circuit breaker is off, (3) light switch failed to close the circuit, (4) light bulb failure (fault), and (5) wiring fault. These constitute what NASA (2002) calls "immediate, necessary, and sufficient" conditions for the fault to occur.

Maintaining a more inclusive description at each level (e.g., naming the components or subsystems and subsequently their failure conditions) results in a fault tree that is more likely to encompass all the detailed mechanisms in lower levels. In contrast, an analysis that jumps directly to causes such as a "burned-out (light bulb) filament" or a "switch malfunction" is equivalent to jumping to conclusions and does not represent the small-steps approach.

The failure mechanisms identified for "circuit breaker off" are (1) the circuit breaker is faulty (failed in the open [off] position), (2) the circuit breaker is activated (tripped) due to excessive current draw, or (3) the circuit breaker was inadvertently turned off. By focusing on reasons for why "the circuit breaker was activated (tripped)," the following causes might be identified: (1) wiring fault (shorted) occurred, (2) too many devices were plugged into the circuit, or (3) a defective device was plugged into the circuit.

Qualitative fault trees can be useful in that they can provide insights regarding logical causes of faults and failure mechanisms. The fault tree can be converted from qualitative to quantitative by proceeding with the following steps.

Step 3: Assign Event Probabilities

To develop a quantitative FTA, your team will assign probability estimates to all basic, undeveloped, and house events ranging from 0.00 to 1.00. Whenever possible, estimates should be based on available data, such as from call centers, complaint databases, or previous usability tests.

How can we develop a quantitative fault tree when no data are available?

A major advantage of FTA is that it can provide insight into the interaction of multiple elements of both system operation and human behavior with regard to likelihood of failure, as it incorporates the normal operations, faults, and logical operators that lead to a top-level event. It is this aspect that gives FTA the ability to estimate the overall probability of failure in a quantitative fault tree.

To achieve a quantitative result, event probabilities must be provided that reflect actual or estimated data. What can you do if data are not available and the team is unsure about providing estimates?

A hybrid approach. The following enables semiquantitative estimates to propagate from qualitative judgments. After your team develops the fault tree, this approach proposes the following steps: (a) assign qualitative probability ratings to all events, (b) substitute preassigned quantitative values for the qualitative values, and (c) calculate the top-level event.

For this example, we will use three qualitative event probabilities—high, medium, and low—rating each event in the fault tree. You would then substitute the numeric values (0.1, 0.01, or 0.001) shown in the third column of the following table for each of the qualitative ratings. In this example, probabilities were chosen to represent conservative (or pessimistic) failure rates, rates that would almost certainly be unacceptable as top-level probabilities. Your team could choose the number of categories and associated probabilities as they deem appropriate.

Probability of Failure	Description	Assigned Value
High	Likely to fail	0.1
Medium	Medium likelihood to fail	0.01
Low	Least likely to fail	0.001

With the event probabilities entered, you would then calculate the top-level probability.

In a robust system, the combinatorial probabilities may show a surprisingly low probability for the top-level event. If the resultant probability is too high, the team should inspect the tree to (a) review estimates of events and make sure they are reasonable and adjust as necessary, (b) explore opportunities for further mitigation by adding those to the fault tree, (c) recalculate probabilities to determine the effect on top-level event probability, and (d) iterate until acceptable levels are achieved. If the result is at or below your preestablished acceptance level, the fault tree could be deemed complete.

Step 4: Calculate the Probability of Each Gate Leading to the Top-Level Event

Fault tree probabilities propagate upward from the bottom-most events. In Figure 4.4, both AND and OR gates are shown with two inputs of identical probabilities: .01. Use of the formulas results in the OR gate probability of failure of about .02 (2 in 100), while the AND gate probability is .0001 (1 in 10,000). If you use automated tools, they do these calculations for you.

When developing and viewing fault trees, it is instructive to note that modes of control will exist as inputs to AND gates, whereby two or more events must occur simultaneously for the fault (failure) to occur. As a result, multiple events on the input side of an AND gate

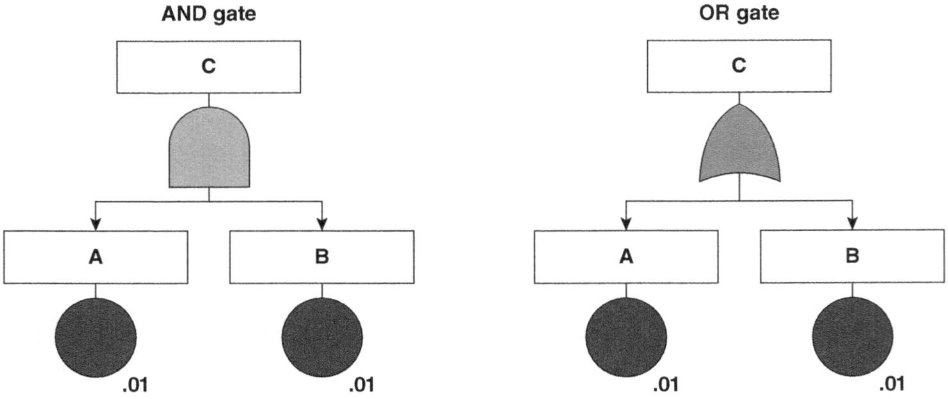

AND gate probability with n input events:
$P(C) = P(A) * P(B) \ldots * P(n)$

Example:
$P(C) = .01 * .01 = .0001$

OR gate probability with n input events
$P(C) = P(A) + P(B) \ldots + P(n) - [P(A) * P(B) \ldots * P(n)]$

Example:
$P(C) = .01 + .01 - .0001 = .0199 \cong .02$

Figure 4.4. AND gate and OR gate with two input event probabilities and computed output. Formulas are shown for nth *input events.*

will, if the probability of the input event is < 1.0, act to decrease the probability of failure. In contrast, multiple events in an OR gate will be additive (minus the product of the inputs) and increase the probability of failure.

Step 5: Determine If the Top-Level Event Probability Is Lower Than the Acceptable Threshold

You should determine acceptability based on predefined criterion levels of probability within your organization. If the probability of the top-level event is acceptable, no further work is needed. If, however, the probability is considered not acceptable, go to Step 6.

In a quantitative FTA, how do we determine whether a given fault probability is acceptable?

A unique characteristic of a quantitative FTA is that it yields the probability of the top-level hazard (event). If the probability is considered to be too high, mitigations can be applied to reduce the overall probability.

Your company or team may have preexisting criteria or policies for making such decisions. If not, how is an acceptable level determined? One possible approach is borrowed from Six Sigma, a widely used set of tools and techniques for process control and process improvements. Six Sigma proposes that when a process is mature or a product is properly designed, the system will operate within prescribed boundaries (6 sigma) 99.99966% of the time, equivalent to a defect rate of 3.4 defects per million opportunities (a probability of 3.4×10^{-6}).

To calculate the probability of an event, determine the number of occurrences of the event divided by the number of opportunities for it to occur. The numerator of the proportion is the threshold "acceptable" number of occurrences, and the denominator is an estimate of the number of opportunities or exposures a device has to exhibit a particular usability fault.

As an example, suppose your firm is developing a device with an anticipated 10-year life span that will have a distribution of 500 units. You assume it is possible for the usability issue being assessed to occur at any time and that the probability does not decline over time (admittedly a pessimistic set of assumptions). Each device is expected to be used about 5 times per day, 250 days per year. From these estimates, the total number of times (opportunities) the total population of devices would be used during the 10-year period is about 6.25 million (500 [devices] × 5 [uses per day] × 250 [days used per year] × 10 [years]. Based on the rate of 3.4 defects per million, about 21 errors would occur during the lifetime of the device. Responsible parties (e.g., the risk management team or project managers) would have to decide whether this is an acceptable number. If the event results in a potentially catastrophic outcome, the failure rate may be judged to be too high and that further design mitigations are required. If the event yields minor consequences, this number could be deemed acceptable.

Step 6: Identify Controls That Will Reduce the Probability of Occurrence

Mitigations to be considered here are the same controls as those discussed in the descriptions of FMEA. Document each mitigation in the fault tree (usually depicted in an AND gate).

Step 7: Determine If New (Use-Related) Hazards Have Been Introduced

While applying changes to the user interface that mitigate a use-related fault, it is possible for a new fault to be introduced into the system that can result in a "cure" that is worse than the "disease." Be sure to consider the possibility of such regression effects whenever you introduce control mitigations.

Step 8: Reassess/Recalculate Gates Affected by New Controls and Recalculate the Top-Level Probability

After you have applied mitigations and other adjustments, recalculate the fault tree.

Step 9: Repeat Steps 6–8 Until Top-Level Probability Is Reduced to an Acceptable Level

Iterate the process of identifying mitigations and assessing the effects on probability until the top-level probability is reduced to at or below the threshold acceptance level.

Uses for Quantitative Fault Trees

Although fault trees are useful when no probability estimates are incorporated, it can be beneficial to estimate probabilities, as we describe in the next sections.

Hazard Probability

Probabilities derived from fault trees can be used as independent analyses or as a supplement to FMEAs. In this case, you could use an FTA as a decision tool to assist your design teams in determining if additional modes of control are needed for further risk reduction, especially when dealing with combinatorial aspects of multiple events or mitigations. After you incorporate new modes of control into the fault tree, you can use revised probability estimates to determine the effect on overall probabilities.

Critical Path Analysis

One of the most useful attributes of a fault tree can be realized by tracing high-probability pathways through the tree. Such a technique, even using qualitative ratings or crude estimates of probability, may uncover high-risk pathways or sensitivities, showing events and causes that require mitigations to reduce such pathways that otherwise may have been overlooked.

Sensitivity Analysis

Performing exploratory exercises by substituting different probabilities for individual events or faults and observing the effect on the top-level probability can be an effective means of assessing system strengths and vulnerability. For example, suppose your team was concerned about an input fault in an FTA that has an estimated probability of .001. To assess the sensitivity, you might replace the value of .001 with 1.00. If the top-level probability changes by a small percentage, this suggests that the selected fault is well controlled. On the other hand, if the top-level probability increases significantly, this could indicate that the system is vulnerable to that particular fault and you should consider further modes of control.

When using one of the FTA software programs on the market, you will find it relatively straightforward and gratifying to perform the substitutions and see the results instantly. If you are not using one of these programs, rather than performing calculations manually, you could also enter the fault tree logic gate operations (formulas) into a spreadsheet. Once the formulas are entered, calculating "what-if" values would be straightforward.

Table 4.2. Advantages and Disadvantages of Fault Tree Analysis

Advantages	Disadvantages
1. Graphical format enables visualization of combinations of events. 2. FTA enables estimation of overall probability of failure based on estimates of basic and other events. 3. Fault trees can be developed using common flowchart drawing tools.	1. Drawings can become large and unwieldy in complex systems. 2. Mitigations are not always explicit. 3. Requires more training than FMEA. 4. Special software is required for rapid development of fault trees. 5. Estimates of probability are required when little to no data exists. 6. Severity is not included and therefore does not fully estimate risk.

Advantages and Disadvantages of Fault Trees

Table 4.2 summarizes the advantages and disadvantages of fault trees. Probably the most important attribute of fault trees is that the graphical representation of events with associated logic gates can provide unique insights into how multiple individual events or failures can lead to or prevent an undesired event. In contrast, FMEAs are framed to focus on single faults and not the combination of events that must occur to contribute to a hazard. The single faults entered into an FMEA are often relatable to lower-level events of an FTA.

A disadvantage of fault tree analysis is that it estimates the probability of failure but not the severity. As such, it does not fully characterize risk as we have defined it earlier (occurrence × severity). That said, a fault tree for a given hazard with a high probability does not necessarily mean that the given event has a concomitant high risk. In fact, an event with trivial consequences (i.e., low severity)—even with high probability—may result in low risk. For this reason, we suggest that you use FTA in conjunction with FMEAs, performing FTAs on moderate- to high-severity faults or in situations when insight is needed involving a combination of faults or events.

Although fault trees can become very large and unwieldy when characterizing complex systems, FTAs remain superior to FMEAs for visualizing the interactions of multiple fault conditions. So even when using FTA as a secondary tool, you should consider it for specific items that are particularly complex or contentious. The case studies shown in Chapters 5 and 6 will further illustrate the use of FTAs.

5 uFMEA and FTA for a Hypothetical Automatic External Defibrillator (AED)

AED Case Study

Chapters 3 and 4 introduced two of the main methods for conducting use error risk analysis: FMEA and FTA. To help you better understand these methods, in Chapters 5 and 6, we present hypothetical narratives of human factors risk analysis processes during the development of two medical devices: an automatic external defibrillator, or AED (Chapter 5), and a self-monitoring glucose meter (Chapter 6). These examples are intended to illustrate the kinds of decision-making processes that teams are likely to encounter during the risk management process.

What Is an AED?

An automatic external defibrillator is a portable device designed to treat a person having a sudden cardiac arrest (SCA). During use, an AED will monitor electrical impulses from the heart and detect the heart impulses for two types of abnormal heart rhythms (arrhythmias) associated with SCA: ventricular fibrillation (quivering heartbeat) and ventricular tachycardia (very rapid heartbeat). When either arrhythmia is detected, the AED delivers, automatically or on command, an electrical charge (commonly referred to as a "shock") across the heart through electrodes placed on the patient's chest. The current that flows across the heart causes a depolarization of the heart muscles and can enable the heart to reestablish a normal rhythm or sinus rhythm. The use of CPR combined with an AED can more than double the chances of survival for a person who has had SCA.

How quickly an AED is used to treat an SCA victim is a vital determining factor for the victim's survival. According to the American Heart Association (2013), "For every minute that passes without CPR and defibrillation, the chances of survival decrease by 7–10%." After 10 minutes, the chances of survival without using an AED are virtually zero unless the body has been cooled to a very low temperature, and even then, survival is not possible after several hours have elapsed (AED Superstore, 2017).

Installation Sites

AEDs are installed in a wide variety of private and public locations, including office buildings, schools, warehouses, factories, airports, sports venues, vehicles, shopping centers, and commercial airliners. They can be used indoors or outdoors in varying weather conditions. AEDs are also being prescribed for in-home use for people with known heart conditions.

AED User Population and Training

Many first responders, such as law enforcement officers, firefighters, and paramedics, are equipped with AEDs and typically receive formal training on their use. In other environments, such as private offices, retail businesses, and exercise facilities, selected personnel are typically given device training and certified to use the device.

One of the most challenging aspects of AED design is that they are commonly installed in public settings, where the assumed user could vary in terms of age, gender, education, language capabilities, medical sophistication, and other characteristics. Advancements in AED usability have been largely responsible for the placement of these devices in

Table 5.1. AED User Profile Includes Medical Caregivers and Lay Users (Trained and Untrained)

	User Group (U.S. Population)		
User-Related Characteristics	**Medical Users**	**Lay User (Key Operators with Training)**	**Lay User (General Population)**
Type of facility	Facility with medical office containing doctor and nurse, or person with EMT training. User able to treat personnel within facility.	Facility with one or more AEDs installed. Facility may have medical personnel but has assigned personnel trained in use of AED.	Facility with one or more AEDs installed. Facility often has no medical personnel. Assume anyone in facility has access to AED.
Age	21–65+	18–65	15–75+
Education/ medical training	Doctors: MD degree LVN: 2-year college RN: 4-year college EMT: EMT certification	High school In-service training on AED	No medical training
Physical stature range	5th percentile female to 95th percentile male	5th percentile female (age 18) to 95th percentile male	5th percentile female (age 15) to 95th percentile male
Vision	Corrected vision to 20/40 vision or better (assume onset presbyopia starting at age 40)	Corrected vision to 20/40 vision or better (assume onset presbyopia starting at age 40)	May be visually impaired (degree of accommodation TBD)
Hearing	Normal hearing (assume high-frequency loss above age 40). Use of hearing aids possible.	Normal hearing (assume high-frequency loss above age 40). Use of hearing aids possible.	Could have hearing impairment (degree of accommodation TBD).
Primary language	English	English, Spanish (other TBD)	English, Spanish (other TBD)
AED training	In-service training	In-service training	None

public places. Medical device regulators expect new AEDs to demonstrate (through usability test data) that they can be used effectively within predefined time limits by first-time target users. Most lay users are likely to have minimal or no training on the device.

For this case study, we will assume that the company has performed field research and established the characteristics for three target user populations: medically trained users, device-trained lay users, and untrained lay users (see Table 5.1).

Design Challenge/Initial Design Assumptions

AED designers have a daunting challenge. An AED must operate reliably in a wide variety of environments despite the fact that they are stored or displayed for long periods of no activity. When needed, the devices must be immediately operable. Perhaps the most challenging aspect is that operating the AED must be so "intuitive" or self-evident that it will enable people with no medical background to use it on a person as quickly as possible—when every second without treatment lessens the probability of success.

In our case study, the AED project is assumed to be in the concept phase, so the detailed design work has not yet been completed. The user needs, preliminary requirements, and general design features (shown next) have been established. Early risk analysis, as part of the usability/human factors engineering process, will be based on the following assumptions, which could change as the design progresses and the risk analysis mandates.

- The unit will be compact, maximum weight 10 pounds.
- It will be enclosed in a metal case to enhance durability and reliability, with a bright color to enhance visibility.
- The device will have a color display measuring 5 inches diagonally (minimum). The display will present EKG information (for medical users), textual and graphical instructions, and warnings. The display will be readable in a range of illumination from darkness to daylight.
- The number of controls will be minimal. "Buttons" on the screen will be enabled with a touch screen.
- Auditory information and warnings will be provided by an internal speaker using simulated voice output and other warning sounds.
- Visual and auditory messages will be configurable in multiple languages to accommodate different marketplaces. Plug-in memory modules will be installed at the factory and can be retrofitted in the field.
- Electrodes to be applied to the patient's chest will be connected to the AED with plug-in conductors. Electrodes will be packaged in easy-to-open sealed envelopes.
- The device will use rechargeable or disposable batteries packaged in cartridges.

AED Preliminary Hazard Analysis

The risk management team had reviewed predicate device records and other sources related to AEDs. With historical records and a review of the new product functions, the team created a list of hazards and related scenarios. One of the most valuable resources accessed by the team was the FDA MAUDE database mentioned earlier. Two example events extracted from the database are shown in Table 5.2. The preliminary hazard analysis is shown in Table 5.3.

Development of uFMEA for the AED

The following describes what we think is a representative depiction of an FMEA development for the AED. In the process, we will try to show the kinds of decision-making that are likely to take place within the context of the FMEA steps described earlier.

Step 1: Perform a Task Analysis

Our team had varying experience with AEDs, so we gave ourselves homework assignments to view online video demonstrations of previous AEDs from our company and others from competitors. We also viewed user manuals and brochures for the leading AEDs.

Our moderator started the team on a step-by-step analysis of the tasks for preparing and using the AED. Because the AED was in early development, some of the design details were not yet determined, so the team based several tasks on existing devices. We developed the

Table 5.2. Example of AED Medical Device Reports Extracted from MAUDE Database

Report Number	Event Type	Mfg.	Date Rev'd.	Brand Name	Event Text
[redacted]	Death	[redacted]	[redacted]	[redacted]	Event Description: THE CUSTOMER REPORTED THAT DURING A PATIENT EVENT, THEIR DEVICE WAS AUTOMATICALLY REVERTING TO AED MODE FROM MANUAL MODE, WHICH WAS CAUSING THE DEVICE TO DUMP DEFIBRILLATION ENERGY. THIS OCCURRED DURING THE EVENT WHEN ATTEMPTING TO DELIVER DEFIBRILLATION ENERGY TO A PATIENT. THE PATIENT DID NOT SURVIVE THE EVENT. THE PATIENT WAS REPORTED TO WEIGH BETWEEN (B)(6). Manufacturer Narrative: (B)(4). THE THIRD PARTY SERVICE AGENT EVALUATED THE DEVICE AND OBSERVED PROPER DEVICE OPERATION THROUGH FUNCTIONAL AND PERFORMANCE TESTING. THERE WAS NO DEVICE ISSUE OBSERVED. THE DEVICE WAS RETURNED TO THE CUSTOMER FOR USE. MANUFACTURER XXX PERFORMED A REVIEW OF THE DEVICE KEYLOG FILE ALONG WITH THE DOWNLOADED PATIENT EVENT RECORD. THIS REVIEW CONFIRMS THAT, DURING THE FIRST 13 MINUTES 39 SECONDS OF USE, THE DEVICE USER REMOVED THE DEFIBRILLATION CHARGE 5 (FIVE) TIMES BY PRESSING EITHER THE CHARGE OR ENERGY DOWN BUTTONS. THE DEVICE USER ALSO SWITCHED TO THE MANUAL MODE 4 (FOUR) TIMES DURING THIS PERIOD OF TIME AND DELIVERED 3 SHOCKS IN THE MANUAL MODE. AFTER THE FIRST 13 MINUTES 39 SECONDS OF USE, THE DEVICE USER USED THE DEVICE IN THE MANUAL MODE FOR THE REMAINDER OF THE PATIENT CALL AND DELIVERED 11 ADDITIONAL DEFIBRILLATOR SHOCKS TO THE PATIENT. MANUFACTURER XXX HAS DETERMINED THAT THE USE ERROR OCCURRING DURING THIS EVENT MAY HAVE CONTRIBUTED TO THE DEATH OF THE PATIENT. MANUFACTURER XXX HAS SENT AN OFFER TO PROVIDE ADDITIONAL TRAINING REGARDING THE USE OF THE DEVICE.
[redacted]	Death	[redacted]	[redacted]	[redacted]	Event Description: COMPLAINANT ALLEGED THAT WHILE ATTEMPTING TO DEFIBRILLATE A (B)(6) MALE PATIENT, THE ELECTRODES WOULD NOT ADHERE TO THE PATIENT'S SKIN AND THE ASSOCIATED DEVICE WAS UNABLE TO OBTAIN AN ECG SIGNAL. COMPLAINANT INDICATED THAT THE CLINICIAN OBTAINED ANOTHER SET OF ELECTRODES TO CONTINUE TREATING THE PATIENT. COMPLAINANT INDICATED THAT THE PATIENT SUBSEQUENTLY EXPIRED, UNKNOWN IF IT WAS A RESULT OF THE REPORTED MALFUNCTION. Manufacturer Narrative: XXX CORPORATION HAS RECEIVED THE PRODUCT AND WILL BE PROVIDING A SUPPLEMENTAL REPORT WHEN OUR INVESTIGATION IS COMPLETED.

Note: Confidential information is blacked out.

Table 5.3. AED Preliminary Hazard Analysis

Hazard	Contributing Events (Including Use Errors [UE])	Hazardous Situation(s)	Harm
AED shock functionality (nondelivery)	• Caregiver failed to press shock button (UE) • Caregiver unable to operate AED (UE) • Improperly placed electrodes (UE) • Failure of arrhythmia detection • Failure of high-voltage system • Battery failure	• Failure to deliver defibrillating shock	• Death • Brain damage (anoxia)
Timing of AED shock delivery	• User delayed while reading instructions (UE) • User delayed when attempting to apply electrodes (UE) • User confusion on how to operate (UE)	• Delay in delivery of defibrillating shock	• Death
AED shock delivered when not appropriate	• Caregiver failed to check patient (breathing, unresponsiveness) (UE) • Failure of arrhythmia detection circuitry	• Administration of shock when not needed	• Death shock-induced arrhythmia
AED shock functionality (ineffective)	• Failure of high-voltage charging system • Damaged pads, conductors	• Delivery of low-energy shock	• Death
AED shock functionality (causes damage)	• Patient in or near flammable liquid (possible UE) • Fire ignited by defibrillator	• Fire (ignited by defibrillator)	• Burns
AED shock functionality (energy not used therapeutically)	• Caregiver or bystander touching patient during delivery (UE) • Failure of auditory system or visual display warnings	• Caregiver or bystander shocked	• Burns, tingling sensation
AED shock functionality (failure to deliver shock after patient relapse)	• User removed electrodes (prematurely) after apparent patient recovery (UE) • Premature battery failure	• Failure to deliver shock during recurrence of arrhythmia	• Death

flow chart shown in Figure 5.1, which shows the task sequence (tasks and subtasks) for the user as well as the automated sequences of the AED.

Step 2: Start a Worksheet

We created a worksheet with the headers and column header definitions shown in Table 5.4. The first column (A) was reserved for an item identifier, a number that is permanently

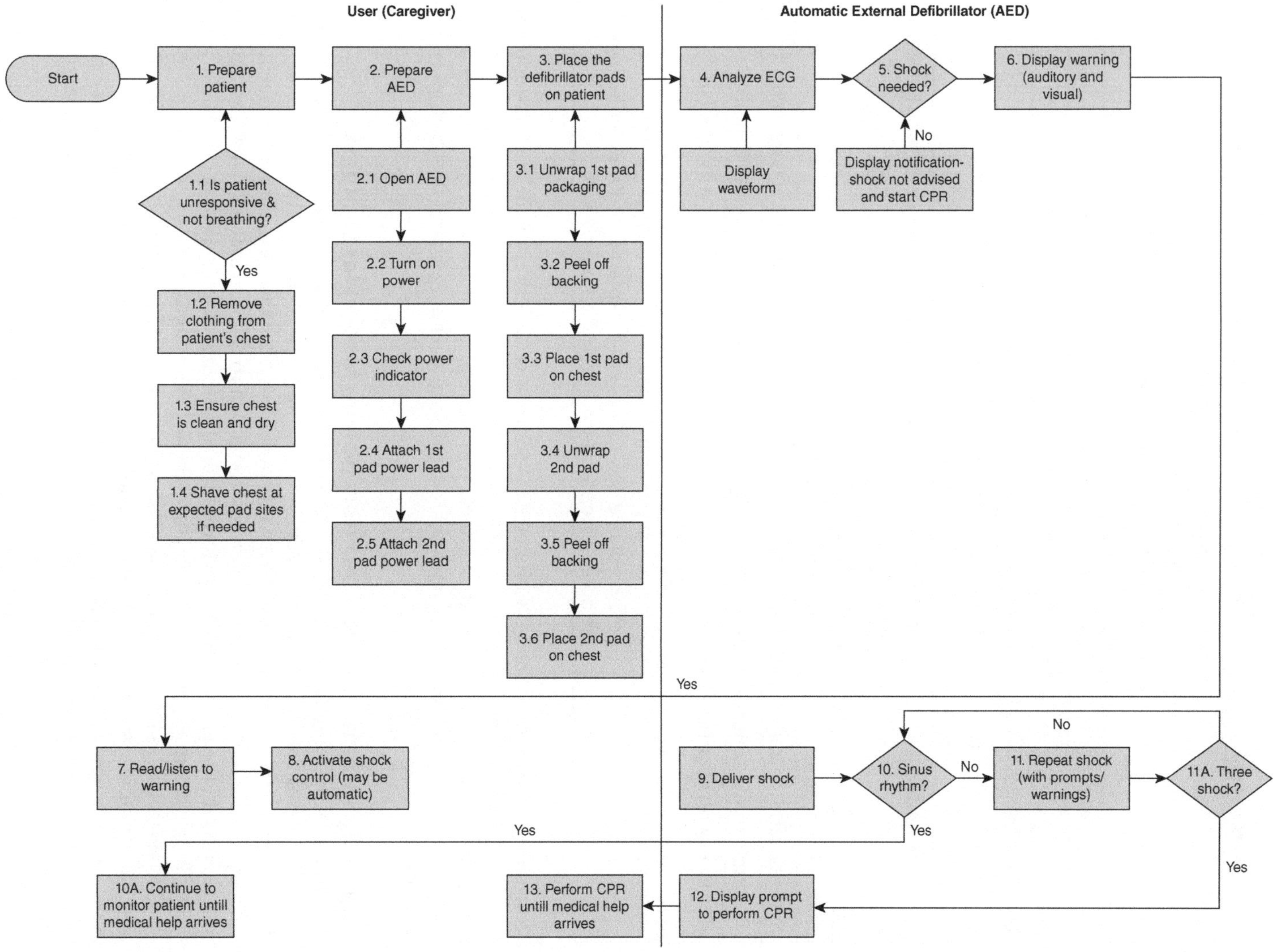

Figure 5.1. AED task analysis.

Table 5.4. FMEA Worksheet Headings and Definitions

Column Header	Description
ID #	Number assigned to each failure mode (use error) for quick reference. This number should remain with the item even when the list is sorted in nonsequential order (e.g., as when sorting by priority or other).
Task/function	Task or function in which error/failure occurred.
Hazard	Potential source of harm.
Use error (failure mode)	Description of the error or failure mode.
Occurrence (use error probability)	Estimated probability of occurrence leading to harm.
Hazard severity	Measure (rating) of the consequences of the hazard, the severity of harm.
Risk level	Combination of occurrence and severity.
Method of control	Description of mitigation for error.
Severity with control	Consequence of hazard after method(s) of control is applied.
Occurrence with control	Probability of occurrence after method(s) of control is applied.
Risk level with control	Combination of occurrence and severity after the method(s) of control is applied.
Acceptability	Assessment of the final risk level. For this example, a high rating is not acceptable, low ratings are acceptable, and medium ratings are acceptable as long as justification is provided.

assigned to each failure mode. Column B provides a description of the task grouping to which the task belongs. Both of these identifiers serve as shorthand for the team when referring to specific failure modes, which will be especially useful when the list is re-sorted and no longer shown in sequential (or task) order. Other column designators will be described in later sections.

Step 3: Brainstorm Potential Use Errors (Failure Modes) for Each Task

We began by examining the subtasks associated with the first task and brainstormed possible errors for each subtask. While reviewing each step, we thought about what difficulties or errors a user could have while performing the task or subtask. We decided to consider errors of omission and commission that led to these questions: what task or part of a task could the user forget to perform or inadvertently skip (omission), and how could the task be performed incorrectly or with difficulty (commission)?

We were also reminded to think about varying task environments and scenarios as well as a variety of users (in this case, we considered all three user groups in Table 5.1). Each team member wrote their thoughts on sticky notes and submitted them to the moderator. Notes were gathered, grouped by category, placed on a wall, and subsequently reviewed by the team.

Example results of the brainstorming sessions are shown in Table 5.5. In Subtask 3.2—the user will "peel off backing from 1st pad"—the first use error identified was "user did

Table 5.5. Example List of Use Errors Identified During First Round of Brainstorming, Listed by Task and Subtask

Task	Subtask	Possible Use Errors/Difficulties
Task 1: Prepare patient	1.1 Check patient—determine if unresponsive and not breathing	"User observed that patient was unresponsive but tried to treat with AED even though patient was breathing and had normal EKG."
	1.2 Remove patient clothing from chest	"User had difficulty removing female undergarment."
	1.3 Ensure chest is clean and dry	• "Raining/moist environment caused chest to remain wet after wiping." • "Excessive sweating."
	1.4 Shave chest at anticipated pad sites	• "Laceration caused by razor." • "Shaved wrong site. Have to shave another area."
Task 2: Prepare AED	2.1 Open AED (cover)	• "Couldn't open the latch." • "Broken fingernail while trying to open latch." • "Unable to determine top-side of unit, tried to open with case upside-down."
	2.2 Turn on AED	• "User did not know when to turn on power." • "Couldn't find the power switch." • "User pushed the wrong button." • "Did not know how to turn on." • "Attempted to turn the switch the wrong way." • "While attempting to turn switch on, found it was already in the on position." • "There doesn't have to be a switch—the device can turn on automatically." (Note: potential design solution.)
	2.3 Check power Indicator	• "Didn't check to see if device is on." • "User couldn't see the power indicator." • "User couldn't tell if the device was activated." • "User did not know what to do next." • "Battery dead, no indicator turned on."
	2.4 Attach 1st pad power lead (connect to AED)	• "User failed to plug in lead (forgot, unable)." • "Damaged lead when attempting to connect to AED." • "Plugged pad connector into the opposite pad receptacle." (Note: polarity doesn't matter; however, ambiguity may cause user confusion and delays.)
Task 3: Place the defibrillator pads	3.1 Unwrap 1st pad packaging	• "User unable to open package." • "User had difficulty opening package—took too long." • "Damaged pad while opening package." • "User attempted to open package with knife or other tool, causing damage to pad." • "Using pads with expired date."
	3.2 Peel off backing from 1st pad—possible use errors	• "User did not attempt to pull off backing." • "Unable to peel off backing." • "Did not remove all of the backing." • "Damaged pad while attempting to peel backing."

not attempt to pull off backing," an omission use error. Errors of commission included "Unable to pull off backing," "did not remove all of the backing," and "damaged pad while attempting to pull off backing."

Some of the identified use errors were based on the team's assumptions regarding the not-yet-finalized user interface. For example, our starting assumption was that there would be a switch for powering on the device. Differences in what team members assumed regarding the power switch design led to different use errors. In a later version of the FMEA, we combined several of the errors associated with a power switch into one statement: "User had difficulty operating the power switch." This nonspecific description helped to later focus on the design and trade-offs of the power-activating mechanism.

After each of the brainstorming sessions, the moderator sorted the errors (and other potential problems) by task and subtask. These items were transferred to the worksheet and presented to the team for review. Table 5.6 shows the initial FMEA worksheet with use errors entered in Column C.

Step 4: Identify Potential Effects of Each Use Error/Failure Mode

In this step, we entered descriptions of the potential harm that could result from the failure mode in column D of the worksheet. When multiple harms could occur for a given failure mode, we listed the most severe effect. While brainstorming, we discovered some new hazards and updated the hazard analysis.

During our brainstorming discussions, among the examples we considered were hazards related to failure to deliver shock to the heart (e.g., ID numbers 3, 4, 7, 10, 12, and 14–16). Such a failure would prevent the shock that would have enabled the heart to resume normal sinus rhythm, likely resulting in death or serious injury (for example, anoxia causing brain damage).

Step 5: Assign Severity Ratings for the Harm

In this step, for each of the potential effects described in column D, we rated the severity in column E. The definitions for severity that we used in the FMEA are shown in Table 5.7.

For group sessions regarding severity estimates, we required that the medical group attend our team meetings so their input would accurately reflect the medical implications of any failures. Here are some examples of severity ratings and accompanying reasoning.

- "Failure to provide shock" (e.g., numbers 3, 4, 7, 10, 12, and 14–16) were rated as major because the nondelivery of shock to a patient would almost certainly lead to death or permanent serious injury.
- Failures involving "delay of therapy" (e.g., numbers 2, 6, 9, 11, and 13) were rated moderate.

We recognized that the risk of death increases with any increment of delay. However, for most items, the team estimated that most delays would be relatively small (in seconds, perhaps), not meriting major severity. We also realized that the accumulation of small delays could result in an overall delay that would be significant enough to reduce the probability of reviving the patient. The team agreed to temporarily rate "delay of therapy" as having moderate severity and decided to postpone final judgment until we could receive the results of preliminary usability tests. Any delays that were observed to be more significant than expected (threshold time to be determined) would be changed in severity from moderate to major.

Table 5.6. Excerpt of Initial FMEA Worksheet with Use Errors and Ratings Shown in Order of Task Analysis

A	B	C	D	E	F	G	H	I	J	K	L
ID #	**Task**	**Use Error (Failure Mode)**	**Effect (Harm)**	**Hazard Severity**	**Occurrence**	**Risk Level**	**Method of Control**	**Severity w/Control**	**Occurrence w/Control**	**Risk w/Control**	**Acceptability**
1	Prepare patient	Tried to treat unresponsive patient with normal sinus rhythm.	Inducement of cardiac arrest or arrhythmia	Major	Occasional	Medium					
2		Difficulty removing female undergarment.	Delay of therapy	Moderate	Occasional	Medium					
3		Raining/moist environment caused chest to remain wet. Pad does not adhere.	Pad not adhered—failure to provide shock	Major	Occasional	High					
4		Excessive sweating, pad does not adhere.	Failure to provide shock	Major	Rare	Medium					
5		Cut skin while shaving chest.	Laceration	Moderate	Occasional	Medium					
6		Shaved wrong site. Required re-shave.	Delay of therapy	Moderate	Occasional	Medium					
7	Prepare AED	User did not know when to turn on power—did not attempt.	Failure to provide shock	Major	Rare	Medium					
8		Difficulty opening latch, slight delay.	Broken fingernail	Minimal	Rare	Low					
9		Unable to determine top side when opening.	Delay of therapy	Moderate	Rare	Low					

(*continued*)

Table 5.6. Excerpt of Initial FMEA Worksheet with Use Errors and Ratings Shown in Order of Task Analysis (*continued*)

A	B	C	D	E	F	G	H	I	J	K	L
ID #	**Task**	**Use Error (Failure Mode)**	**Effect (Harm)**	**Hazard Severity**	**Occurrence**	**Risk Level**	**Method of Control**	**Severity w/Control**	**Occurrence w/Control**	**Risk w/Control**	**Acceptability**
10		User did not know when to turn on power—did not attempt.	Failure to provide shock	Major	Occasional	High					
11		User had difficulty operating power switch.	Delay of therapy	Moderate	Occasional	Medium					
12		Found switch was already in the on position. (Inadvertently left on—battery dead.)	Failure to provide shock	Major	Occasional	High					
13		User couldn't determine if AED was turned on.	Delay of therapy	Moderate	Rare	Low					
14		No indication of power when activated—battery dead.	Failure to provide shock	Major	Probable	High					
15		User failed to connect pad lead (forgot, unable).	Failure to provide shock	Major	Occasional	High					
16		Damaged lead while attempting to connect.	Failure to provide shock	Major	Occasional	High					

Note: Letter designators for each column are used as quick references only and not part of the table.

Table 5.7. Severity Ratings and Definitions for the AED

Severity Rating	Consequences
Major	The hazard could directly result in death or serious injury of the patient or operator.
Moderate	The hazard could directly result in moderate injury to the patient or operator.
Minimal	The hazard is not expected to result in negative medical consequences or any complication.

Table 5.8. Probability of Occurrence Ratings and Definitions for the AED

Probability of Occurrence	Description
Probable	Likely to occur regularly or many times during the life of the product under specified operating conditions.
Occasional	Likely to occur infrequently or several times during the life of the product under specified operating conditions.
Rare	Will rarely occur or is very unlikely to occur during the life of the product under specified operating conditions.
Improbable	Not expected to occur under specified operating conditions.

Step 6: Estimate Occurrence (Probability) of Use Error Leading to Harm

In this step, we had to remind ourselves that this is not just the probability of the error but also the probability of the error leading to the harm. One of four probability ratings (improbable [lowest], occasional, rare, or probable [highest]), defined in Table 5.8, were entered into column F for each use error in the worksheet.

Our strategy was to assign the extreme labels to items judged to have very high or very low probabilities. Specifically, this meant that probable ratings were those that were expected to happen with regularity (virtually certain), and improbable ratings were assigned to those that never (or hardly ever) happen. The middle ratings of occasional and rare tended to require more discussion.

Step 7: Assign a Risk Index

In the worksheet we used the severity and occurrence ratings for each failure mode to determine the risk index ratings to be entered in column G. This step required no judgment, as the risk indices were predefined by the levels of occurrence and severity in Table 5.9.

Table 5.9. Risk Index Definitions Used for the AED

	Hazard Severity		
Probability of Occurrence	Major	Moderate	Minimal
Probable	High	High	Medium
Occasional	High	Medium	Low
Rare	Medium	Low	Low
Improbable	Low	Low	Low

Step 8: Prioritize the Failure Modes (Use Errors) by Risk Level

At this point, the FMEA worksheet characterized preliminary risk levels for each use error before mitigations were applied. To prioritize the failure modes, we sorted the list by risk level in descending order (high to low), shown in Table 5.10.

Step 9: List the Method of Control (Mitigations) for Each Failure Mode/Use Error

Our next task was to brainstorm mitigations for each use error. These were entered in column H. The following is an example of the team discussions regarding risks and mitigations.

For the use error "AED battery dead (power inadequate to complete multiple defibrillation attempts)," we identified two instances in which the battery had inadequate power, causing a failure to complete defibrillation (IDs 12 and 14). In the case of ID 12, the power switch was inadvertently left on, and for 14, there was no indication that the power was on.

Initially, we identified three potential causes for dead battery: a defective battery or charging system, an old (outdated) battery, and the AED power switch was inadvertently left on, causing the battery to drain. To mitigate the risk of a dead battery in a facility, we initially proposed four features. Of those, items b and c in the following list are mitigations commonly used in the industry.

a. Provide a second (backup) battery with circuitry that would automatically switch from primary to backup battery when the primary battery falls below a preset voltage.
b. In a way similar to smoke alarms, provide an auditory alarm that would sound and periodically provide an alert that the unit needs attention, signifying that the battery needs to be charged or replaced.
c. Provide a label on each battery that specifies an expiration date, after which the batteries should be changed regardless of the charge state.
d. To prevent the power being left on inadvertently, we proposed the elimination of a conventional power switch. Instead, power would be activated when the AED cover was opened and turned off when closed.

Step 10: Determine If New Hazards Have Been Introduced or If Estimated Risks for Other Hazards Have Been Affected

In our initial discussions of the AED sequence for shock delivery, we assumed that when the AED was ready to administer the shock (arrhythmia detected and high-voltage circuits charged), the user would be prompted to press the shock button, and presumably do so in a timely manner—a scheme commonly used in existing AEDs. An advantage of the user-activated shock control is that the caregiver or user can ensure that no one is touching the patient before pressing the button.

However, the team was concerned about two failure modes that had the potential to harm the patient. The first was related to "delays in activating shock control" (ID 31), and the second was "failure to activate the shock button" (ID 32). We had assigned these failure modes occurrence ratings of occasional and rare, respectively, resulting in medium risk for both. We proposed an alternative scheme that reduces or eliminates the risk of delays or failure to press the shock button by changing the shock delivery control from manual to automatic. When the conditions are met for shock delivery, the AED would

(text continued on page 66)

Table 5.10. Excerpt of uFMEA Table for the Hypothetical AED

A	B	C	D	E	F	G	H	I	J	K	L
ID #	**Task**	**Use Error (Failure Mode)**	**Effect (Harm)**	**Hazard Severity**	**Occurrence**	**Risk**	**Method of Control**	**Severity w/Control**	**Occurrence w/Control**	**Risk w/Control**	**Acceptability**
3	Prepare patient	Raining/moist environment caused chest to remain wet. Pad does not adhere.	Failure to provide shock	Major	Occasional	High	Waterproof adhesive. Rain kit (contains towels, cover) for wet environments.	Major	Rare	Med	Accept w/ justification
10	Prepare AED	User did not know when/ how to turn on power—did not attempt.	Failure to provide shock	Major	Occasional	High	Automatic power activation w/cover open. Voice and visual prompts.	Major	Improbable	Low	Accept
11	Prepare AED	User difficulty operating power switch.	Delay of therapy	Moderate	Occasional	High	Automatic power activation w/cover open.	Moderate	Improbable	Low	Accept
14	Prepare AED	Battery dead, no power indication.	Failure to provide shock	Major	Probable	High	• Automatic activated backup bat. • AED stored bat expiry date. • Mandatory periodic inspections. • Auditory alarm on low bat or bat expiration. • Internet-based AED inspection reminder/ record keeper and messaging alert sys. • Automatic mechanical flag alarm. • Cell-based alert sys (TBD).	Major	Improbable	Low	Accept w/ justification

(continued)

Table 5.10. Excerpt of uFMEA Table for the Hypothetical AED (*continued*)

A	B	C	D	E	F	G	H	I	J	K	L
ID #	**Task**	**Use Error (Failure Mode)**	**Effect (Harm)**	**Hazard Severity**	**Occurrence**	**Risk**	**Method of Control**	**Severity w/Control**	**Occurrence w/Control**	**Risk w/Control**	**Acceptability**
15	Prepare AED	User failed to connect pad lead (forgot, unable).	Failure to provide shock	Major	Occasional	High	Pads are connected prior to use during install/ maint.	Major	Improbable	Low	Accept
16	Prepare AED	Damaged lead while attempting to connect.	Failure to provide shock	Major	Occasional	High	Pads are connected prior to use during install/ maint.	Major	Rare	Med	Accept w/ justification
17	Prepare AED	Confusion on whether leads can be reversed.	Delay of therapy	Moderate	Occasional	High	Pads connected prior to use—install/maint.	Moderate	Improbable	Low	Accept
20	Place pads	Damaged pad while opening package.	Failure to provide shock	Major	Occasional	High	Easy open packaging—usability test.	Major	Improbable	Low	Accept
25	Place pads	Pad did not adhere to chest (patient + environmental moisture).	Failure to provide shock	Major	Occasional	High	Waterproof adhesive, rain kit, shaving kit, towels in kit.	Major	Improbable	Low	Accept
21	Place pads	Pad used past expiration date.	Hard to adhere pad	Moderate	Occasional	High	Expiration recorded in AED. Mechanical flag activated on expiry.	Major	Improbable	Low	Accept
22	Place pads	User failed to pull off backing completely.	Inadequate shock	Major	Occasional	High	Large tab on easy-pull backing—usability test req'd.	Major	Improbable	Low	Accept

Table 5.10. Excerpt of uFMEA Table for the Hypothetical AED (*continued*)

A	B	C	D	E	F	G	H	I	J	K	L
ID #	**Task**	**Use Error (Failure Mode)**	**Effect (Harm)**	**Hazard Severity**	**Occurrence**	**Risk**	**Method of Control**	**Severity w/Control**	**Occurrence w/Control**	**Risk w/Control**	**Acceptability**
23	Place pads	User damaged pad/connection while removing backing.	Failure to provide shock	Major	Occasional	High	Large tab on easy-pull backing—usability test req'd.	Major	Improbable	Low	Accept
24	Place pads	Placed pad in wrong part of chest.	Failure to defibrillate	Major	Probable	High	AED visual instructions w/illus. Diagrams on pad packs.	Major	Rare	Med	Accept w/ justification
25	Place pads	Pad did not adhere to chest (adhesive old).	Inadequate shock	Major	Occasional	High	Waterproof adhesive—extended longevity. Expiration date + alarm.	Major	Rare	Med	Accept w/ justification
26	Place pads	Pad placed on chest, pulled off to reposition. Did not adhere.	Failure to provide shock	Major	Occasional	High	Specify and test pads for 3 successive applications. Provide backup pads.	Major	Rare	Med	Accept w/ justification
27	Shock needed? No shock advised.	User fails to perform CPR when "no shock advised" by AED.	Failure to oxygenate	Major	Occasional	High	Visual and auditory instructions provide how-to and packaging info.	Major	Rare	Med	Accept w/ justification
2	Prepare patient	Difficulty removing female undergarment.	Delay of therapy	Moderate	Occasional	High	Provide safety scissors for cutting straps.	Moderat	Improbable	Low	Accept

(*continued*)

Table 5.10. Excerpt of uFMEA Table for the Hypothetical AED (*continued*)

A	B	C	D	E	F	G	H	I	J	K	L
ID #	Task	Use Error (Failure Mode)	Effect (Harm)	Hazard Severity	Occurrence	Risk	Method of Control	Severity w/Control	Occurrence w/Control	Risk w/Control	Acceptability
4	Prepare patient	Excessive sweating, pad does not adhere.	Failure to provide shock	Major	Rare	Med	Waterproof adhesive with extended life. Expiration date alarm/ flag.	Major	Improbable	Low	Accept
5	Prepare patient	Cut skin while shaving.	Laceration	Moderate	Rare	Med	Provide safety razor with easy-open foam.	Moderate	Improbable	Low	Accept
6	Prepare patient	Shaved wrong site. Required re-shave.	Delay of therapy	Moderate	Occasional	Med	AED visual instructions. Diagrams on pad packs.	Moderate	Rare	Low	Accept
7	Prepare AED	User did not know when to turn on power—did not attempt.	Failure to provide shock	Major	Rare	Med	Automatic power activation w/cover open.	Major	Improbable	Low	Accept
12	Prepare AED	Found switch was already in the on position. (Inadvertently left on—battery dead.)	Failure to provide shock	Major	Occasional	Med	Automatic power activation w/cover. See dead bat.	Major	Rare	Med	Accept w/ justification
18	Place pads	User unable to open package.	Failure to provide shock	Major	Rare	Med	Easy-open packaging—usability test.	Major	Improbable	Low	Accept
19	Place pads	Difficulty opening pad packaging.	Delay of therapy	Moderate	Occasional	Med	Easy-open packaging—usability test.	Moderate	Improbable	Low	Accept

Table 5.10. Excerpt of uFMEA Table for the Hypothetical AED (*continued*)

A	B	C	D	E	F	G	H	I	J	K	L
ID #	**Task**	**Use Error (Failure Mode)**	**Effect (Harm)**	**Hazard Severity**	**Occurrence**	**Risk**	**Method of Control**	**Severity w/Control**	**Occurrence w/Control**	**Risk w/Control**	**Acceptability**
28	Do not touch patient—warning	User or bystander does not hear warning.	Burns, induce arrhythmia	Moderate	Occasional	Med	Automatic gain control provide margin of loudness over ambient noise level.	Moderate	Rare	Low	Accept w/ justification
29	Do not touch patient—warning	User or bystander does not see warning.	Burns, induce arrhythmia	Major	Occasional	Med	Large, bright visual display w/pullout shade. Auditory warnings.	Major	Rare	Medium	Accept w/ justification
30	Do not touch patient—warning	User or bystander does not understand warning.	Burns, induce arrhythmia	Major	Occasional	Med	Visual and auditory warnings provided in multiple languages.	Major	Rare	Medium	Accept w/ justification
31	Activate shock control	User delays in activating shock control.	Delay of therapy	Major	Occasional	Med	Automatic shock activation with warning.	Major	Rare	Medium	Accept w/ justification
32	Activate shock control	User fails to activate shock button.	Failure to provide shock	Major	Rare	Med	Automatic shock activation with warning.	Major	Improbable	Low	Accept
1	Prepare patient	Tried to treat unresponsive patient with AED. Patient has normal sinus rhythm.	Possible inducement of arrhythmia	Major	Occasional	Med	AED tests for specific arrhythmia before shock is administered.	Major	Improbable	Low	Accept

Note: Letter designators for each column are used as quick references only and not part of the table.

initiate visual and auditory warnings, and the shock would be activated without further user intervention.

Although automatic shock activation would reduce the risk of hazards associated with manually pressing the shock control, we realized that another hazard was made more likely: the risk that a caregiver or bystander might receive a shock from contact with the patient (IDs 28, 29, and 30). With the manual control sequence, the user could make sure that everyone is "clear" (not touching the patient) before activating the shock button. But with the automatic shock control, the avoidance of shock will be dependent on the effectiveness of auditory and visual warnings. To mitigate the possibility of failed warnings, we proposed enhancing both visual and auditory warnings to make them more salient and difficult to ignore. The team recommended that extensive usability studies be performed to ensure the effectiveness of these warnings.

There remained some doubt that we could completely eliminate the possibility of contact with the patient during shock delivery. Fortunately, while reviewing the literature, we found evidence to indicate that the severity of receiving a shock from contact with a patient may not be as life-threatening as we had assumed. Hoke, Heinroth, Trappe, and Werdan (2009) performed an analysis of defibrillator usage involving 29 adverse events in which people received inadvertent shocks. The results indicated no accounts of life-threatening conditions or long-term disability. The team agreed that this information, combined with confirmatory usability test results and the fact that other manufacturers have also employed automatic shock delivery, was enough to justify that the remaining risk was acceptable.

Step 11: Assess the Effect of Mitigations on Risk Level (Determine Residual Risk)

Column K displays the postmitigation residual risk. Comparing the premitigation severity and occurrence ratings in columns E and F with the same ratings in I and J will indicate whether the changes in risk are due to changes in severity, occurrence, or both.

For example, for ID 3, the failure mode ("raining/moist environment . . . pad does not adhere") was initially rated as a high risk (major severity with occasional occurrence). The residual risk (after the application of controls) was rated medium, with a reduction of occurrence from occasional to rare.

Step 12: Assess Whether or Not Residual Risk Levels Are Acceptable

The designations of whether the residual risk levels in column K were acceptable are shown in column L. The criteria for acceptability were predefined by the example shown in Table 3.8. The table defined the acceptability of low, medium, and high residual risk; low being acceptable; medium, acceptable with justification; and high, not acceptable.

Example of residual risk not meeting acceptable level. Earlier we described the failure mode ID 14 regarding dead batteries and the proposed mitigations. At that point, we had rated the residual risk as having a rare occurrence and a resultant risk level of medium. In a review of complaint databases, we found that other manufacturers of AEDs on the market had used several measures to reduce the risk of depleted batteries: (a) a low-battery auditory alarm, (b) a battery expiration date, and (c) required periodic inspections (e.g., monthly) of installed units.

Despite these measures, it was apparent that there were a number of recurring instances of battery failure, resulting in AEDs failing to function when attempting to treat a patient. Since the mitigations were similar to and beyond the ones we had proposed, we were compelled to change our previous occurrence rating from rare to occasional, resulting in high residual risk. The following summarizes our discussions.

- *Failure of periodic inspections to discover low or dead batteries.* Although we agreed that periodic inspections seem sensible and reasonable, the team speculated that facilities could occasionally (even frequently) fail to inspect their units due to, for example, forgetting, absence of regimented procedures, changes to personnel assigned to the task, or disruptive events. If inspections were neglected for a long period, even a backup battery would not be able to eliminate the chance of completely depleted batteries in AEDs at the site.
- *Failure of auditory alarms to alert facility.* AEDs typically have an auditory alarm to signal when the battery is low. It is easy to imagine that auditory alarms found in AEDs (e.g., beeper, chime) may not be heard in noisy environments. Auditory alarms could also be rendered inaudible when the devices are housed inside AED display cabinets. The auditory alarm will eventually stop sounding when the AED's battery is no longer capable of powering the alarm.

Additional mitigations to reduce risk. It was apparent that mitigations we had initially proposed for reducing the risk of dead batteries would be inadequate when dealing with the spectrum of users and environments. The following summarizes our discussions related to additional mitigations for addressing the dead battery issue.

- *Enhancement to auditory-only alarm (addition of mechanical alarm).* In addition to enhancements to the auditory alarm (such as automatic gain control, proper frequency selection, and higher amplification), we proposed the implementation of a mechanical indicator that would be revealed when the primary or secondary battery was depleted or had reached its expiration date.
- *AED inspection management system—internet-based application.* The team agreed to add the requirement for periodic inspection of AEDs. To reduce the probability of forgetting to perform these inspections, we proposed the development and deployment of an internet-based application that would help manage routine inspections. This application would have the following capabilities:
    - Automatically send emails and smart phone text messages at configurable dates and times to personnel assigned to AED inspections.
    - Record AED inspection "sign-off"—the application enables a user to certify that an inspection was performed on the date and time indicated. As an optional feature, the sign-off function could be set up to require the inspector to enter a one-time code displayed by the AED.
    - If an inspection was not completed on the scheduled date and time, a reminder would be sent automatically to the key operator(s).
    - If inspections have passed the due date (TBD days), the application would automatically notify a (configurable) list of recipients.
- *Active network for conveying AED information—option 1.* A more advanced mitigation would be to have the AED use its AC power source to keep a network connection via Ethernet cable or Wi-Fi to communicate with a central monitoring system such as the one just proposed. Maintenance personnel would have access to a dashboard.
- *Cell-phone-based link for conveying AED information—option 2.* Another solution proposed that each AED contain a cellular-phone-based link that would store and send the information through the software application described in option 1.

With these mitigations, the team consensus was that the risk of dead batteries in the AED leading to the device's failure to defibrillate would be reduced from high to low (occurrence rating of improbable), as shown in Table 5.10.

Step 13: Repeat Steps 9–12 Until Risks Are at Acceptable Levels

If we had found any remaining items that were rated medium or high (not acceptable), we would have repeated the process to brainstorm additional mitigations to reduce the residual risk to an acceptable or justifiable level.

Fault Tree Analysis for an Automatic External Defibrillator

The following is a depiction of how a risk management team might develop an FTA for the AED. In this example, we illustrate the FTA process, the kinds of decision-making that will be encountered, and the outcomes that might be expected.

The FTA illustrations in this example were developed using a commercially available fault tree analysis software tool (Relyence Fault Tree). Following the FTA steps outlined earlier, we illustrate the stepwise building of a portion of a fault tree, starting from a top-level event and expanding downward to the basic events.

Step 1: Identify the Undesired Event To Be Analyzed (Top-Level Hazard)

The team reviewed the preliminary hazard analysis, which listed the following hazards. For this example, we address item 4: "Caregiver (user) or bystander shocked."

1. Nondelivery of defibrillating shock.
2. Delay in delivery of defibrillating shock.
3. Administration of shock when not needed.
4. Caregiver (user) or bystander shocked (current fault tree example).
5. Fire started by defibrillator.
6. Delivery of weak, ineffective shock.
7. Repeat cardiac arrest episode in same session, AED already removed.
8. Burns caused by electrodes touching each other during high-voltage discharge.

We started the fault tree by drawing the top-level event shown in Figure 5.2. We used an OR gate because we anticipated that there would be multiple causes leading to this fault.

Step 2: Build the Fault Tree

The team brainstormed about ways a user or bystander could get shocked while using the AED. Ideas presented by individuals were recorded on a whiteboard. Here are some of the scenarios that team members identified that could lead to shock of the caregiver or bystander.

- User or bystander was touching the patient and didn't hear the prompt to "clear."
- User or bystander was holding the patient because the patient appeared to be convulsing.
- User or bystander was touching the AED case, and the high-voltage circuit was not properly isolated.
- A non-English-speaking person was attempting to use the AED. The user did not understand the visual and auditory warnings.

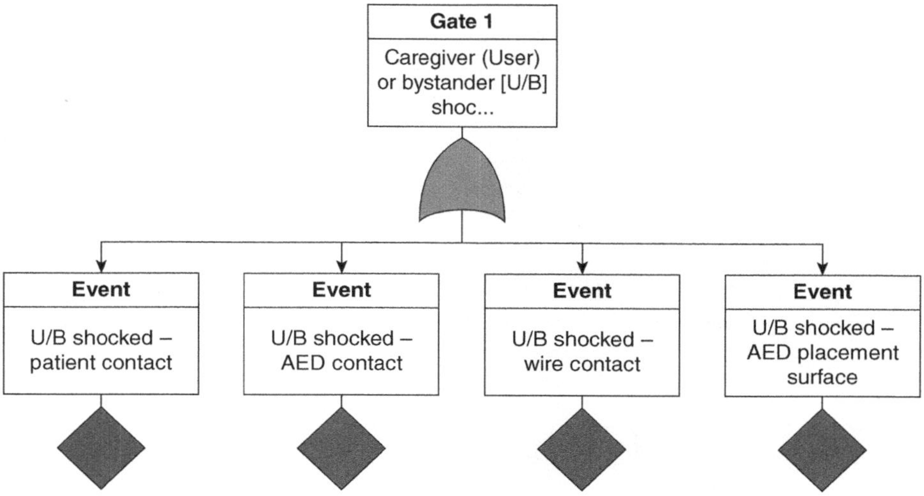

Figure 5.2. Top-level event, OR gate with four input events.

As you can see from this brief list, the causes for a given event can be diverse, including use error, machine failure, and environmental conditions. Some are single events that could lead (directly) to shock (e.g., touching patient during shock administration), and others involve multiple events.

The first round of brainstorming yielded four events that could occur in which the user or bystander could get shocked while using the AED.

- Shocked by contact with patient.
- Shocked by contact with AED.
- Shocked by contact with conductors (leads to pads).
- Shocked by surface on which AED is placed.

The four events were placed as inputs to the OR gate (Gate 1) of the top-level event shown in Figure 5.2.

B. User/bystander shocked by patient contact (Figure 5.3, Gate 2). We chose to develop one branch at a time. The event "User/bystander shocked by patient contact" was developed as the first branch of the fault tree. We focused our events on answers to the question, "What events would have to occur for someone to touch a patient when shock is being administered?" The team started with the following assumptions regarding AED use.

- After the charging circuit is ready, the shock will be activated automatically or when the user activates the shock control (e.g., button).
- An auditory warning (e.g., simulated voice) will sound to warn the user or a bystander not to touch the patient. The auditory warning for users in the United States will be given in English as the default language (other languages can be incorporated).
- The AED display will present a graphical and textual warning directing the user and bystanders not to touch the patient when the shock is to be delivered.

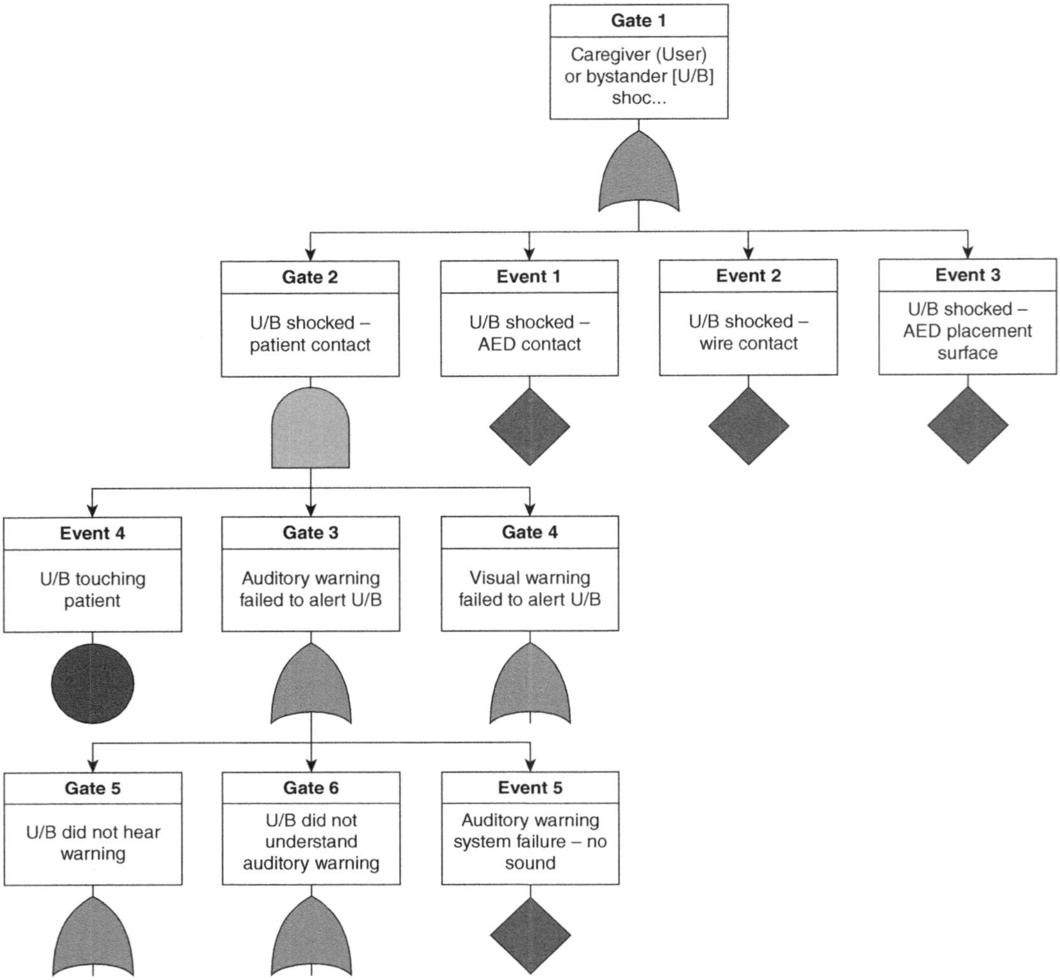

Figure 5.3. Gate 2 "User/Bystander shocked—patient contact" was changed to an AND gate with inputs Event 4, Gate 3, and Gate 4. At Gate 3, "Auditory warning failed to alert user/bystander" is shown to have three causes: Gate 5, Gate 6, and Event 5.

During the brainstorming session, we identified three events that would have to occur for a user or bystander to be shocked by contact with the patient.

1. The user or bystander touches the patient during high-voltage shock delivery.
2. Failure of the *auditory* warning system to alert the user or bystander to refrain from touching the patient.
3. Failure of the *visual* warning system to alert the user or bystander to refrain from touching the patient.

Because all three input events must occur simultaneously for the Gate 2 event to occur, these inputs are shown as inputs into an AND gate (Gate 2) of Figure 5.3. Event 4, "User/bystander touching the patient," was designated as a basic event. The failures of the auditory warning (Gate 3) and visual warning systems (Gate 4) to alert the user or bystander are shown with OR gates, as we anticipated that there would be multiple causes for these events (failures).

A. Auditory warning failed to alert user/bystander (Gate 3). For Gate 3 we asked, "What events could cause the auditory warning to fail to warn the user?" We identified three possible causes:

1. User/bystander did not hear the warning.
2. User/bystander did not understand the warning.
3. Auditory warning system failed—no sound (or below-threshold sound).

These are shown as inputs into the OR gate of Gate 3 (Figure 5.4). Gates 5 and 6 were drawn with OR gates, again anticipating multiple causes for each. The third, "Auditory systems failure" (Event 5), was left as an undeveloped event, as engineering agreed to analyze this event and update it at a later date.

B. User/bystander did not hear the auditory warning (Figure 5.4, Gate 5). Next, we addressed the first of the two potential causes for Gate 5: "User/bystander did not hear the auditory warning." Two potential causes were identified for this failure:

1. User/bystander is hearing-impaired.
2. High ambient noise caused masking of the auditory signal.

These causes are shown as basic events at the bottom of the tree branch (Events 7 and 8).

C. User/bystander did not understand the auditory warning (Figure 5.4, Gate 6). We then brainstormed about reasons why the user/bystander did not understand the auditory warning at Gate 6. The potential causes we identified were as follows:

1. The user did not understand the auditory (voice) warning because it was in English, which was not the user's or bystander's native language.
2. The auditory output of the device was garbled or distorted.
3. The auditory voice message was ambiguous or not appropriate for the user/bystander.

These inputs (Events 9, 10, and 11) are shown as inputs into Gate 6 (lower right corner of Figure 5.4).

Completion of the branch. Similar to the process described for Gate 3, we developed the input branches of Gate 4, "Visual warning failed to alert user/bystander."

The completion of Gates 3 and 4 enabled the completion of Gate 2, shown in Figure 5.5, "User/bystander shocked by patient contact." To complete the fault tree for the top-level event (Gate 1), the team would then develop the branches for Events 1, 2, and 3 (branch development not shown).

This process and the resultant FTA drawings illustrate the developmental progression of a fault tree. The process focuses primarily on the identification of undesirable

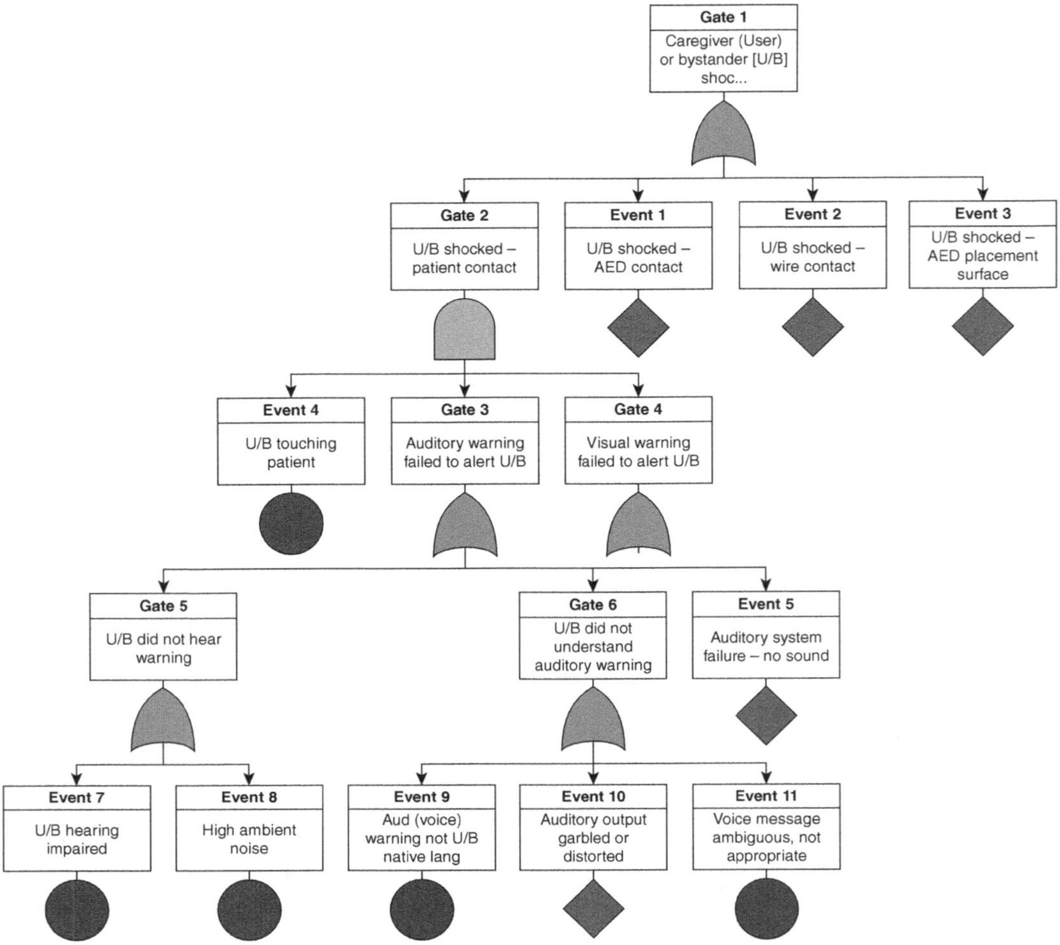

Figure 5.4. Gate 6, "User/bystander did not understand warning," is shown with causes (input Events 9, 10, and 11).

(high-level) events that are decomposed into lower-level events, eventually leading to basic events.

Step 3: Assign Event Probabilities

So far, our FTA has been developed as a qualitative analysis. An FTA can be made quantitative by assigning probabilities to basic and undeveloped events. The probabilities of each gate are calculated according to the formulas shown earlier, with values propagating upward, culminating in the calculation of the top-level event.

Starting at the bottom is necessary when performing manual or spreadsheet calculations. When using an FTA tool, probabilities can be entered in any position or order; however, calculations at each gate cannot be performed until all of the constituent event probabilities are entered.

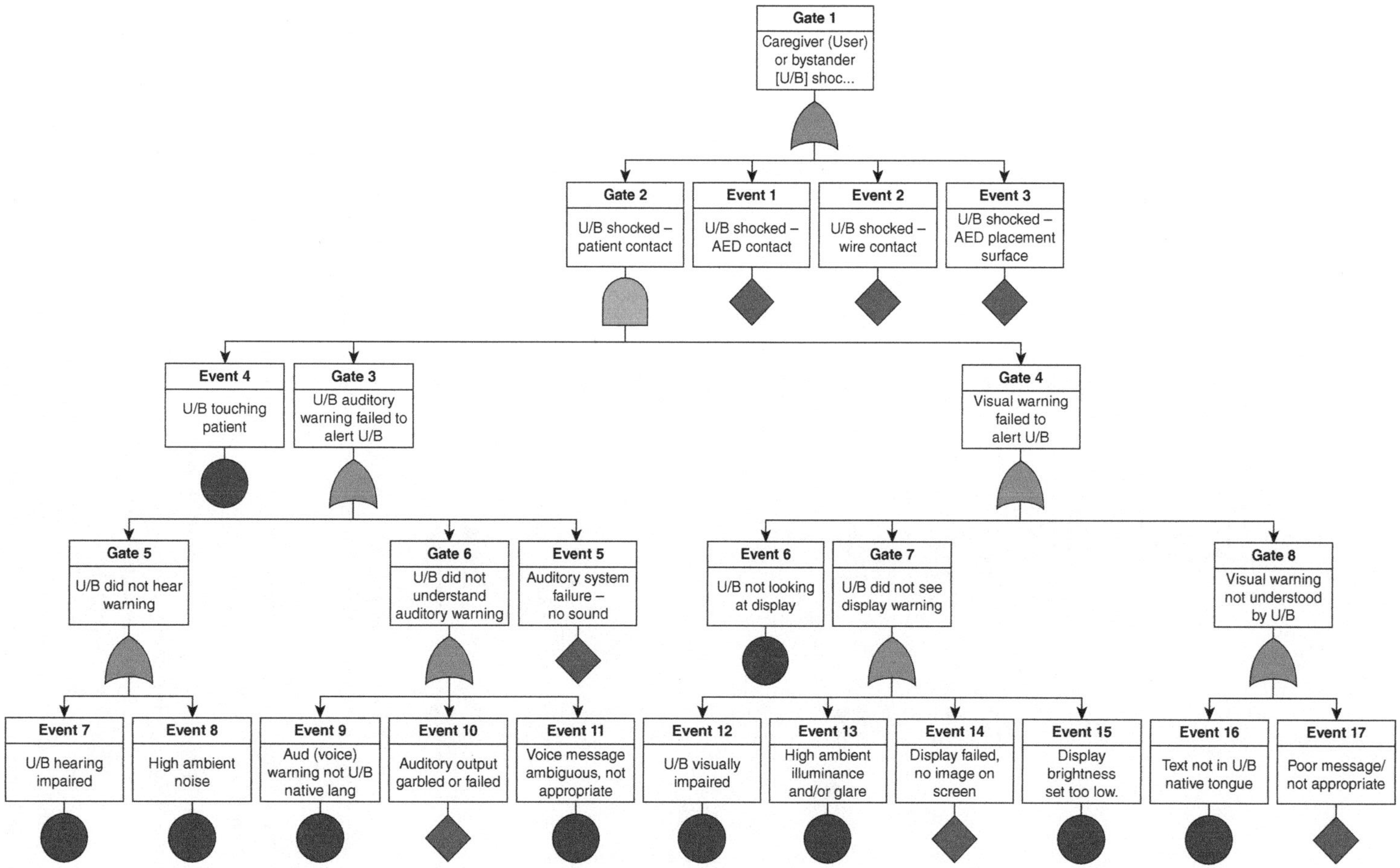

Figure 5.5. Fault tree is completed for Gate 2, "User/bystander shocked by patient contact," with the addition of Gate 4 and associated branches.

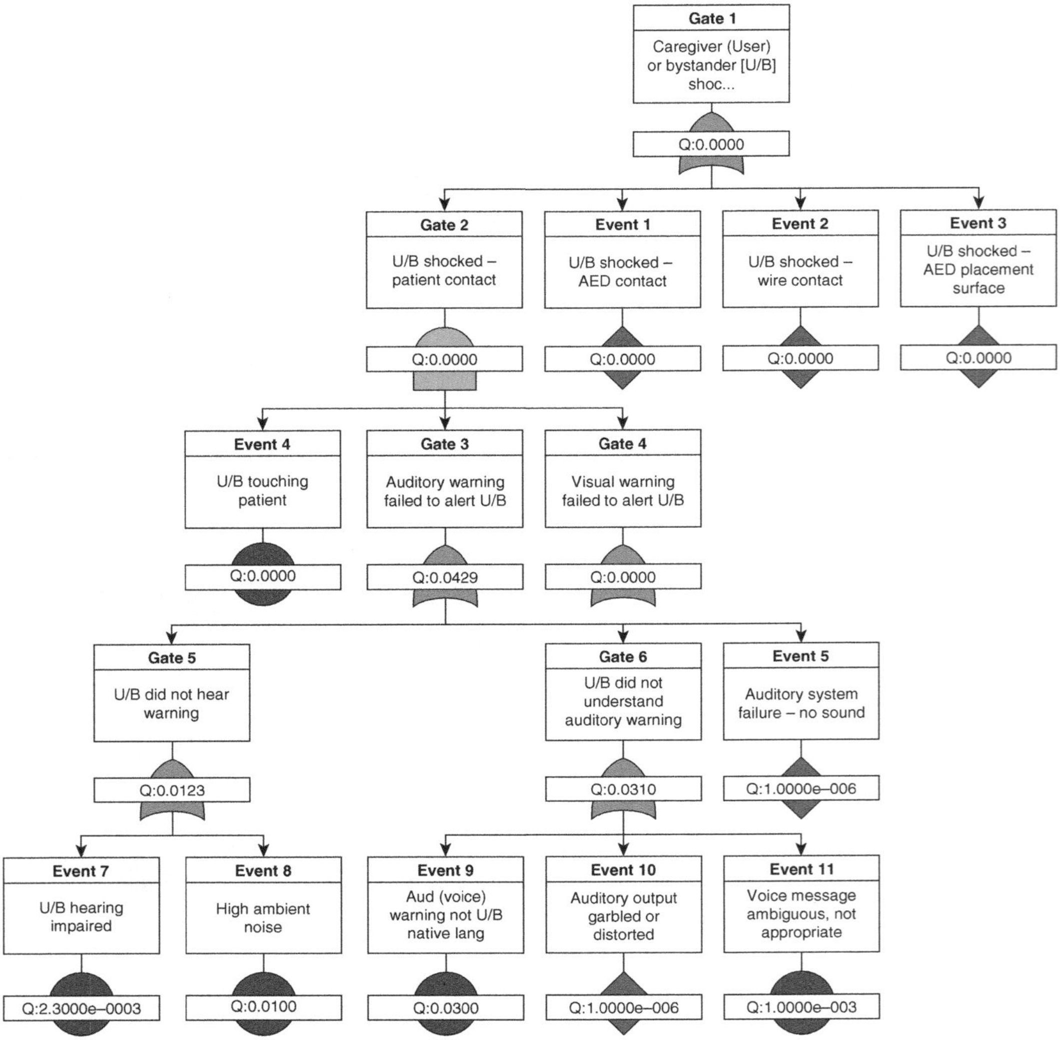

Figure 5.6. Probability estimates for Events 7 and 8 of Gate 5 and Events 9, 10, and 11 (Gate 6) are entered. With inputs from Gate 5, Gate 6, and Event 5, the probability of Gate 3 is calculated.

Starting with the bottom of the tree in Figure 5.6, we estimated the event probabilities for Gate 5 using the following rationale.

- The probability of hearing impairment (Event 7) was derived from the U.S. census report analyzing deaf and hearing-impaired populations. We estimated that the proportion of the population who would not be able to hear and understand an auditory warning was about 0.23% of the total population.
- For Event 8, "high ambient noise" conditions (causing the auditory warning to be masked and not understood), a customer site survey was planned to determine the proportion of installed sites with high-noise environments. The team estimated a probability of .01.

The probabilities were entered into Events 7 and 8 in the FTA, as shown in Figure 5.7.

Step 4: Calculate the Probability for Each of the Gates Leading to the Top-Level Event

When you use an FTA tool, the gate probabilities are calculated automatically. When calculating manually or using a spreadsheet, you would calculate probabilities as described in Chapter 4.

A. Gate 5 ("User/bystander did not hear warning") probability resulting from the above input events is shown in Figure 5.7.

B. Gate 6 ("User/bystander did not understand warning") probability. The input (event) probabilities for Gate 6, shown in Figure 5.7, were entered as follows.

- Event 9, "Auditory (voice) warning not [in] user/bystander native language" probability was derived from an American Community Survey report indicating the proportion of non-English speakers (initially $p = .03$; see later text for the subsequent change).
- Event 10 was based on the component reliability estimate ($p \times 1 \times 10^{-6}$).
- Event 11 was based on an estimate from human factors testing indicting that the warning message was effective and that the probability of failure was estimated at $p = 1 \times 10^{-3}$.

C. Gate 3 ("Auditory warning failed to alert user or bystander" [to not touch patient]). The remaining input probabilities for Gate 3 were entered as follows.

- Event 5: The probability of "auditory system failure" was based on an engineering estimate of 1×10^{-6}. With the inputs for Gate 5 and Gate 6 complete, the inputs for Gate 3 were complete and calculated.
- Change to Event 9 probability: The probability for Event 9 was based on the proportion of non-English speakers, initially 0.03. Adding Spanish to the user interface could reduce the chance of users not understanding the auditory instructions by one third, from 0.03 to 0.02. This changed the probability for Gate 3 from $p = .031$ to $p = .0242$ (shown in Figure 5.7).

D. Gate 2 ("User or bystander shocked by patient contact") (Figure 5.7). Continuing as in the earlier text, after completing calculations for Gate 3 and entering probabilities for the events in Gate 4 and Event 4, we were able to calculate the probability of Gate 2. Notice that while the inputs for Gate 2 (Event 4, Gate 3, and Gate 4) show relatively high probabilities of .01, .0242, and .0437, respectively, the output of Gate 2 shows the combinatorial effect of the AND gate: about 1.06×10^{-5}.

Step 5: Determine If the Top-Level Event Probability Is Lower Than the Acceptable Threshold

Ordinarily, the top-level event (Gate 1) would be completed after developing fault tree branches for Events 1, 2, and 3. For illustrative purposes, let's assume for now that each of the events has a probability of 0.00. By doing so, we can examine the contribution of the branch developed above (Gate 2) on the top-level probability (Gate 1).

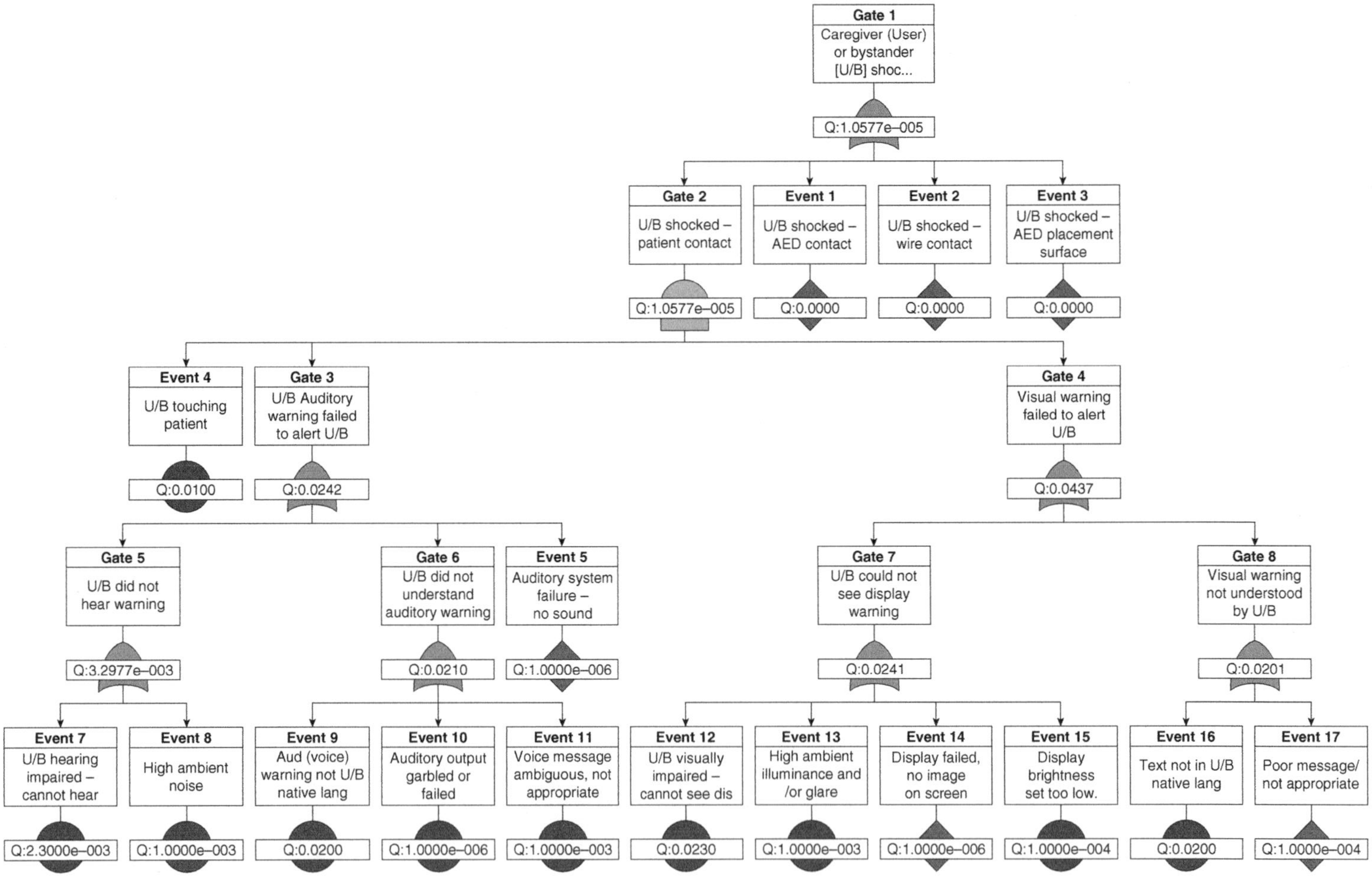

Figure 5.7. Gate 2 probability. With the values available for Event 4, Gate 3, and Gate 4 (and temporarily setting the probabilities of Events 1, 2, and 3 to 0.00), the probability for Gate 2 (the top-level gate) is calculated.

In its current state, the Gate 1 probability (~1.06×10^{-5}) would not have met the criterion set by the team, which is one part per million (1.0×10^{-6}).

Step 6: Identify Controls That Will Reduce the Probability of Occurrence

Gate 2 (AND gate) of this FTA depicts the conditions that must occur simultaneously to cause a caregiver (user)/bystander to be shocked by contact with the patient. One approach for reducing this probability is to find a mitigation that would act in parallel with the other inputs (added to the AND gate).

For example, suppose engineering developed a hypothetical module that could sense when a patient is being touched (for example, by sending a low-voltage test current through the electrodes and measuring current leakage). If the system sensed that the patient was being touched, the AED would suspend the shock and activate a loud auditory warning as well as show an animated warning that they should remove their hands from the patient. The addition of a touch detection module would be represented in the FTA as a touch detection failure—an added input to AND Gate 2 (not shown). Even with a rather pessimistic failure rate of .01, the resultant probability of Gate 1 would change from 1.06×10^{-5} to 1.06×10^{-7}.

Step 7: Determine If New (Use-Related) Hazards Have Been Introduced

No new hazards were found. However, the team remained watchful for any potential issues from the proposed mitigations. We would pay attention to expert review and usability test results to discover any unanticipated issues.

Step 8: Reassess/Recalculate Gates Affected by New Controls and Recalculate the Top-Level Probability

After the high-probability events have been examined and mitigations and other adjustments have been applied, the fault tree is recalculated, as described in the earlier examples.

Step 9: Repeat Steps 6–8 Until Top-Level Probability Is Reduced to an Acceptable Level

If the probability of occurrence is lower than your threshold criterion, you can claim that the probability has been reduced to an acceptable level, at which point the fault tree is complete. If, however, the probability remains above the acceptance threshold, you must continue to look for mitigations that will reduce the top-level probability.

6 Additional Case Study: Blood Glucose Meter

This chapter contains another case study to illustrate some additional principles and methods for conducting a human factors–focused risk analysis. The case study pertains to a hypothetical blood glucose meter, a medical device that employs small samples of blood from finger pricks to analyze and measure glucose levels.

Both Type I and Type II diabetics need to monitor their levels of blood glucose to properly control their disease. They need to keep that level in a controlled range so it is not too low in order to prevent hypoglycemia, which can lead to coma or death, or too high, causing hyperglycemia, which, in extreme cases, can lead to coma or death or cause cumulative damage to multiple organs or limbs. Blood glucose is controlled by either injecting insulin to reduce levels or taking glycogen (or the equivalent) to raise levels.

With the hypothetical glucose meter, users would be able to

- display a reading on blood glucose level from a sample of blood taken from small pin pricks to the skin,
- input the number of carbohydrates taken during meals and snacks during the day and when they were consumed,
- input when and how long the user exercised during any particular day,
- input information about other health-related issues, such when they are feeling ill,
- input when and how much insulin or glucagon they have taken, and
- get a dosage recommendation for how many units of insulin they should take, especially associated with meals or other daily events.

Common use scenarios for a blood glucose include the following.

- Set up the meter for the first time.
  - Set time and date.
  - Set units of measure.
  - Activate carbohydrate-counting feature.
  - Activate meal-marking time.
  - Activate features that allow tracking of events such as exercise and illnesses.
- Get a blood sample and obtain a glucose reading.
  - Insert a strip into the glucose meter.
  - Use a lancet device to prick a fingertip or other part of the body—including alternative sites such as the forearm, abdomen, or thigh—to obtain a drop of blood.
  - Apply the blood to a glucose strip.
  - Read the glucose meter after it processes the blood sample.

For purposes of this case study, these are the main user groups and their profile characteristics.

1. Diabetic patients who are very diligent in obtaining readings, counting carbs, marking mealtimes, and recording exercise and other health-related events.
2. Diabetic patients who do not regularly check their glucose levels multiple times per day and occasionally deviate from fixed insulin doses that are preset for each meal based on carb counts and other activities.

3. Diabetic patients who are very casual in taking glucose readings and do not count carbs with each meal. They do the bare minimum to keep their glucose levels in the target range specified by their doctor.

Task Analysis

As we noted in earlier chapters, the foundation of a solid risk analysis is to perform a robust and comprehensive task analysis. A detailed task analysis was performed for this glucose meter case study. The tasks and subtasks flow from the high-level use scenarios, to be described. A more complete description of the tasks from the task analysis would be done and documented in a use FMEA.

Risk Analysis

This section describes the risk analysis for the glucose meter, including (a) a hazard analysis, (b) a use FMEA, and(c) a URRA (use-related risk analysis).

Hazard Analysis

We conducted a high-level hazard analysis for the glucose meter case study. It covers the most obvious and significant hazards. As described in the AED case study, this is a top-down analysis of hazards that can become hazardous situations through a possible sequence of events, which could include use errors. These hazardous situations can then lead to harm.

The most significant harm that can result from misuse of a glucose meter is diabetic coma and death. Other serious harms include brain and other organ damage. This hazard analysis is an important next step that typically is done after completing a task analysis. Both are important inputs to the more comprehensive use-related risk analysis, which typically has been a use-related FMEA and sometimes fault tree analysis.

uFMEA for a Glucose Meter with Insulin Dose Indications

Next, we look at a partly completed uFMEA for the glucose meter, which normally would have a detailed list of tasks, subtasks, or steps. This is meant to be illustrative for this second, abbreviated case study; it is not meant to be exhaustive. Unlike the AED risk analysis case study, we are not showing all the intermediate steps in getting to a complete uFMEA.

Following the uFMEA, we present an example of a URRA, which is essentially an excerpt from the uFMEA with annotations in a format highly recommended by the FDA for medical products.

Any uFMEA requires descriptions of the levels of the important variables that are part of risk. There are many methods to estimate and describe risks; the AED case study in Chapter 5 used qualitative (adjectival) descriptions of levels. Specifically, that case study used three levels of harm severity (major, moderate, and minimal), four levels of probability of occurrence (improbable, rare, occasional, and probable), and three levels of risk index (or risk level: high, medium, and low).

For this hypothetical glucose meter with insulin dosage calculation, we illustrate another methodology, using semiquantitative estimates or numeric estimates, which are also widely used by risk analysts. Although use of numerical values is common, we caution that you should never succumb to the false precision that some imply when numerical values are assigned.

The values to estimate overall risk levels are as follows.

- Five levels of harm severity: catastrophic (5), high (4), moderate (3), low (2), and negligible (1).
- Five levels of probability of occurrence of harm. As usual, we need to heed the caution that probability estimates of use error for human behavior are notoriously unreliable. The levels are frequent (5), probable (4), occasional/possible (3), rare/remote (2), and improbable (1).
- A risk chart can be derived that contains three levels of risk index (high, medium, and low) when severity of harm is combined (multiplied) with probability of occurrence.

For semiquantitative ratings, the combination is the same as the product of the two numeric estimates. Risk index values range from 1 to 25. As described in Chapter 3, you should note that these numeric scales are ordinal, not interval scales. Interval scales have equal distances between values, whereas ordinal scales do not. We know that there are issues with multiplying ordinal numbers. Severity = 4 is not twice severity = 2, and probability = 4 is not four times probability = 1. This means that the combinations of severity and probability in a risk chart are not to be considered precise calculations but, rather, simply directional and rational combinations of these variables. But in performing use error risk analysis in this case study, they serve the purpose even though they are not rigorously statistically based.

Residual risk acceptability. These are the risk index values for the hypothetical blood glucose meter that the team established:

- Intolerable: high risk level ≥ 15
- Acceptable with justification or ALARP (as low as reasonably practicable): medium risk level ≥ 8 and ≤ 14
- Acceptable: low risk level ≤ 7.

Table 6.1 shows excerpts from a uFMEA for the glucose meter.

uFMEA (Prioritized by Risk)

Another of the steps for the AED case study was to reorder the uFMEA based on risk index levels. Since this second case study is not meant to be as extensive, we will not create a risk-prioritized uFMEA table, but it is easy to imagine what that would look like. However, in this glucose meter case study, we will do something slightly different: derive a URRA from the data in the uFMEA. As noted earlier, the FDA has stated that URRA is its preferred method for characterizing critical tasks as part of medical device regulatory submission for product approval before it is commercialized.

Use-Related Risk Analysis (URRA)

The main purpose of a URRA is to categorize and describe critical tasks, which are those that lead to harm when a use error is committed. These critical tasks become the focus for designers to improve the user interface to try to design out or reduce the likelihood of use error. Critical tasks are also those that require testing in both formative and, later, summative or validation usability testing. So, identification of critical tasks is very important in designing safe and effective products.

Table 6.1. Use FMEA (Brief Excerpts)

ID #	Task	Use Error (Failure Mode)	Effect (Harm)	Hazard Severity	Occurrence	Risk Level	Method of Control	Severity w/Control	Occurrence w/Control	Risk with Control	Acceptability
Initial meter setup											
1	Turn on meter	User is unable to power on the device	No result or delayed result	4 High	2 Rare	8 Medium	• Single button on device • Two ways to power on device (power/ meter home button or strip insertion) • System labeling provides instruction on how to power on the meter	4 High	1 Improbable	4 Low	Acceptable
6	Set up meter parameters	User does not understand setup is complete	None	2 Low	1 Improbable	2 Low	• Message displayed on home screen: "Meter setup is complete!" • System labeling provides instruction on how to set up the meter	2 Low	1 Improbable	2 Low	Acceptable
Performing a blood glucose test											
9	Obtain a measurement	First-time user: failure to properly apply blood to the side of the test strip	No result or delayed result	4 High	4 Probable	16 High	• Screen displays animation of finger going to side of strip • System labeling provides instruction on how to perform a blood glucose test • System labeling provides troubleshooting information	4 HIgh	3 Occa sional	12 Medium	Acceptable with justification

As noted in Chapter 1, regulators like the FDA are highly skeptical about the reliability of use error occurrence estimates because of the limited ability to predict complex human behavior, including the probability of use error. For that reason, the URRA excludes use error probability estimates and instead focuses on tasks and use scenarios with high severity of harm for mitigation and usability testing evaluation. This thinking dictates what is presented in a use-related task analysis.

Table 6.2 is an example of a URRA for our glucose meter case study. The columns describe the task, the potential use error, the potential harm and its severity, determination as being a critical task, the risk mitigations, and how the mitigations are evaluated.

This URRA example is partly completed for the sake of brevity and to reduce redundancy. It shows only a sample of the critical tasks with the highest severity of harm, level 5 (catastrophic, resulting in death or serious injury). It is common in URRAs to list all the tasks involved in using a device and judging each on whether it meets the criteria for being critical. Determining whether or not to categorize a task as critical sometimes is based on a relative judgment. In the case of a device like this glucose meter, we judge that both severity levels 4 (high) and 5 (catastrophic) should be categorized as critical tasks. Such judgment calls on the part of the team (including clinical experts) conducting this risk analysis would need to be justified.

Another decision in creating a URRA is whether to present the tasks in a logical order following use scenarios of interest or in order of the severity of harm. We prefer the logical task flow order and use it in our abbreviated example, but a team creating a URRA could easily choose other schemes. The most important feature of a use-related risk analysis is that it allows you to identify all critical tasks and when a use error can lead to serious harm or death. A critical task requires special attention in the product design phases to reduce risk and also so the effectiveness of the control mitigation can be evaluated in the final summative validation usability test.

Regulators like the FDA expect that the summative usability test also includes so-called essential (or noncritical) tasks, which are described as tasks that are necessary for using the product that would not normally cause harm when a use error occurs. This gives the FDA a more complete picture of how the product will be used. A major concern with the FDA is that selecting tasks for evaluation in a typical uFMEA in which a team may have made erroneously low estimates of use error probability would result in some tasks of high harm severity being ignored in the design and evaluation of the product. This is thought to be less likely to happen when a URRA is used to identify critical tasks, when the focus is only on severity of harm and ignores the probability of occurrence of use errors.

The FDA does acknowledge in its human factors guidance (FDA, 2016a) that use errors on critical tasks have to be "reasonably foreseeable." Our interpretation is that we can say that some harms may not be reasonable to include; for example, programming an infusion pump when a meteorite strike occurs near the hospital. We argue that there are some circumstances that are not reasonable to include in the analyses.

Discussion

This second, highly abbreviated case study reinforces the principles of how human factors methods can be applied in the process of risk management. It also illustrates that there are slightly different approaches to how the methods may be applied. For example, this glucose meter case study incorporated semiquantitative, or numeric, estimates using five-point scales of the probability of occurrence of use error and the severity of the possible

Table 6.2. Use-Related Risk Analysis (URRA)—Partially Completed with Only the Highest-Severity Critical Tasks

Task #	Use Task Description	Description of Potential Use Errors	Potential Hazards/ Harms and Severity	Critical Tasks (Yes/No)	Risk Mitigation Measure for Each Use Error	Evaluation Method in HF Validation Study
11	Obtaining a blood glucose measurement	User with contaminated hands does not wash hands before performing a blood glucose test	Inaccurate result 5 Catastrophic	Yes	• Screen display animation of hand washing • Labeling warning to wash hands	Scenario 2, Task 2 in validation test
15	Obtaining a blood glucose measurement	User does not understand what to do when seeing message "Low glucose"	Hypoglycemic event 5 Catastrophic	Yes	• "You are low" is a button that can be tapped for more information about what this means and what the user can do. • Warning symbol included with "You are low" and is blinking. • System labeling provides information on understanding your test results including "low glucose."	Scenario 2, Task 4 in validation test
16	Obtaining a blood glucose measurement	User unable to read "Low glucose" message due to hypoglycemic condition (e.g., blurred vision)	Hypoglycemic event 5 Catastrophic	Yes	• Font size of glucose result designed to be larger than all other text, giving the user a better chance of at least seeing the number if not the message. • Blinking caution icon added next to low message. • "You are low" is a button that can be tapped for more information about what this means and what the user can do. • System labeling provides information on understanding your test results.	Scenario 2, Task 4 in validation test
17	Obtaining a measurement	User does not understand what to do when seeing message "High glucose"	Hyperglycemia or diabetic ketoacidosis 5 Catastrophic	Yes	• "High glucose" is a button that can be tapped for more information about what this means and what the user can do. • System labeling provides information on understanding your test results.	Scenario 2, Task 5 in validation test

resulting harm. We have cautioned those who apply these semiquantitative methods to be wary of giving false precision to these estimates, since they are just numbers that can as easily be expressed solely as qualitative adjectives, as was done in the AED case study.

We hope we have expressed the reservations of many analysts that estimations of probabilities of occurrence of use error can be highly unreliable and should be undertaken with great caution. The estimates of probability are best viewed as a barometer of how a risk control mitigation can result in a relative reduction in the estimate of use error probability even when we have low confidence in the actual probability of such error. But the relative reduction in the estimation of use error probability does serve in judging if residual risk has been reduced.

Another method shown in this second case study was the description of use-related risk analysis through the URRA table. This description of risk, as preferred by regulators like the FDA, does not even address the difficult estimation of use error probability and focuses on harm severity and how that is being mitigated in the design and evaluation of a product.

7 Common Mistakes and Additional Considerations for Risk Analysis

Mistakes and Pitfalls in Conducting Use-Related Risk Analysis

The following are challenges often encountered in performing overall and use-related risk management. Failure to consider these mistakes and pitfalls in conducting risk analysis could compromise the utility and ultimate value of the process.

Treating Risk Management as a Necessary Evil Rather Than a Development Tool

With tight development schedules and budgets, it is not uncommon for manufacturers to treat risk management as less important than other activities. Such attitudes can have detrimental effects, such as providing inadequate resources and scheduling for performing proper risk management. Risk management that includes use errors should be thought of as an integral tool in developing a system rather than as a necessary evil. Treating risk management as a checkbox activity will increase the likelihood of developing an unsafe system and could result in denial of regulatory approval.

Delaying Risk Management

Another common perception is that risk management is an activity you can defer until the last minute in development. After all, it would seem a lot easier to perform risk analyses with the design and mitigations complete.

Delaying use error risk management until late in development (or with a completed design) presents two main problems. The most obvious one is that when you are pressured to meet tight timelines, your analysis may be done too hastily (and perfunctorily) to be adequate. The second, and perhaps more important, problem is the loss of opportunity afforded by early assessment. Early in the life cycle, it can be relatively straightforward to incorporate design objectives and elements that can set the direction for mitigating certain risks before the device is completed. As detailed drawings, software, and documentation are developed, resistance to change increases even though the designs may not be finalized. Later in the design life cycle, when hardware is finalized for production and software has undergone extensive testing, it becomes exponentially more difficult and costly to make changes. If a serious potential design flaw in the user interface is discovered that would force a change to the hardware or software design, the cost of design changes and opportunity costs of delay to market will be significantly higher than if the issues had been identified earlier in development.

For this reason, risk management—including use error risk management activities—should be initiated early in the life cycle, starting with initial design concepts, and should be updated throughout the cycle.

Blaming the User

In past years, investigators of accidents or incidents involving misuse of medical devices commonly concluded that the incident was due to human error. If the manufacturer declared that the device was not used properly (misused) and the device or system "functioned as designed," the user was often deemed wholly (or partly) responsible for the incident and the manufacturer was typically declared blameless.

In such cases, a designation of "user error," "operator error," "human error," and the like is often used as a code phrase for placing blame on the user rather than on any deficiencies of the system, training, or instructional materials. Regulatory agencies as well as human factors and usability standards no longer support the automatic designation of user error (blaming the user). Therefore, we employ the term "use error" recognizing that errors can have multiple causes, including inadequate or faulty user interface design.

Unfortunately, blaming the user remains a commonplace attitude and can carry over into use error risk management. Such biases are sometimes manifested when discussion of use error scenarios elicit comments such as "Users aren't that stupid" or "Trained users would never do that." Team members who tend to blame the user might not be able to recognize situations in which user interface design could cause use errors or how design could be used to mitigate errors. Team leaders should discuss such potential biases with the group before starting the analysis and monitor discussions and provide guidance when appropriate.

Underestimating or Overestimating Fault Probability or Severity

In this section, we discuss the consequences of bias in estimating probabilities and severity and how to combat such biases.

Possible consequences of underestimating probability or severity. As we have stated, when objective data are lacking, you will need to depend on estimates of fault probability and severities to estimate risk. When faced with constant pressure to maintain tight timelines and product and development costs, you may unintentionally tend to underestimate the probability or severity of identified faults. A reduction of either or both could reduce the overall risk level for a fault from a level that would have required mitigation to one that does not. In such cases, the opportunity for mitigation could be lost or at least delayed.

If a serious risk was intentionally or unintentionally reduced and an incident involving a fault actually occurred for devices in use, the occurrence may result in severe injury or even death. This is not a situation that any developer would want to experience.

Possible consequences of overestimating probability or severity. On the other hand, the fear of underestimating risk may cause team members to be overly conservative by biasing occurrence or severity of harm ratings upward with the intent of adding a safety margin. Routinely overestimating these risk elements can have its own negative consequences.

- If risks are routinely inflated, it may be difficult to discriminate faults that actually have higher risk from those that have lower risk, thus rendering them difficult to prioritize. In other words, if everything is high priority, the reality is that nothing is high priority.
- Overestimating risk could lead to increases in product costs due to the implementation of unnecessary mitigations. Even if product costs are not directly affected, unnecessary mitigations will almost certainly lead to increased costs due to extended development timelines, increased testing, and delays to market (opportunity costs).
- If risk ratings are frequently inflated, individuals outside your team who are assigned to review your analysis are likely to be alarmed by the proportion of items you have assigned higher risk levels. As they investigate further, reviewers may disagree with various risk ratings. If you cannot justify your judgments, your team will likely have to rereview the analysis. Such actions can be undesirable and could reduce your team's credibility, which could interfere with your group's ability to convince implementers that selected mitigations are necessary.

Ways to combat either under- or overestimation bias. Here are some actions that could be employed to reduce possible estimation bias.

a. *Assemble knowledgeable teams.* Select people who have experience dealing with users of the same or similar devices and who can represent the users' perspective (e.g., clinicians, human factors and customer support personnel).
b. *Empower your team to make independent judgments.* Teams should not be constrained by product management to make risk judgments.
c. *Perform user tests.* Usability studies involving representative users performing tasks on mock-ups or early prototypes are among the most effective ways to objectively assess the user interface's susceptibility to use error.
d. *Provide a preview.* Before turning in the first draft of your risk analysis, ask trusted individual(s) outside your team to provide feedback.
e. *Review identified faults and risk priority with stakeholders.* This should be done before presenting mitigations or their potential impact on costs or schedules.
f. *Use methods that can minimize the effects of group dynamics.* Use techniques for gathering unbiased group estimates such as the Delphi method, as discussed later in this chapter.
g. *Use experts to establish severity ratings.* For medical devices, it is important that your team includes persons with medical or clinical background who are responsible for making qualified medical judgments and can provide justification for severity ratings.

Failing to Document Risks That Were Initially Considered Low

Judgments such as "Users would never do that," noted earlier, may cause your team to quickly discard items that elicit such judgments from the analysis. One resulting problem is that faults that are quickly discarded could have higher risk than initially considered. It could be that simply rewording the fault description or considering a fault under different circumstances could change how the fault is rated.

To guard against this problem, it is safer to retain all identified risks during early brainstorming, even if they are considered very unlikely. Later, when your team rates the probability and severity of faults, you can consider whether a given fault has a low probability or is so unlikely that the fault should be deleted. Erroneously deleting a fault is an outcome we all want to avoid.

Failing to Address Risks Identified in Predicate Devices

When designing a new device based on previous (predicate) devices, it is easy to overlook risks that have been well controlled and perhaps taken for granted. Your team should review predicate device documentation to include all relevant risks and mitigations.

Over-Relying on Training or Labeling

As discussed earlier, a frequently proposed solution for minimizing errors is to provide instructions or place labels or warnings on the device. Because instructions are not always read, remembered, or understood, they are considered less reliable for reducing the chance of error than the design of the user interface. For situations in which labeling or instructions are the main or only means of preventing use errors, they should be tested with representative users (i.e., validated) to ensure their effectiveness.

Failing to Validate Modes of Control

The common method for demonstrating effectiveness and thereby validating the user interface (including instructions and training) is usability testing. This involves testing representative users of the device as they perform representative tasks on the actual device or a reasonable facsimile. Whether the mitigations for an identified use error are dependent on design, labeling, or training, regulatory and standards organizations require the manufacturer to show evidence that the mitigations are effective.

Alternative Terminologies and Approaches to Use-Related Risk Analysis

Regulatory Terminology in Risk Analysis

You will see a variety of terminologies used in this field of use-related risk management. In Chapter 6, we gave an example of a URRA. This FDA-preferred method is in the agency's draft Guidance (FDA, 2018) in Appendix B. An example appears in Table 7.1.

As noted, the emphasis in the URRA table is the severity of harm of potential hazards, when probability of occurrence is not included at all in determining whether or not a task would be considered critical. The mitigation for each task is described as well as the method used to evaluate the effectiveness of the mitigation. We provided an example of a URRA in the glucose meter case study in Chapter 6, Table 6.3.

Another term that appears is "use error risk assessment," or UERA. This umbrella term includes what is traditionally called a use FMEA, use FMECA, or, sometimes, an application FMEA (see Phillips-Medisize & U|Sensus, 2018).

The U.S. Veterans Administration Hospital system has a form of FMEA that it calls "HFMEA," or health care FMEA (DeRosier et al., 2002). It is a variation on the uFMEA and does include the controversial probability of occurrence estimates. The VA has used HFMEA to examine risks for many clinical processes, such as

- executing the discharge of a patient from a VA hospital,
- monitoring blood glucose as part of a clinical care plan,
- observing patient flow through the Emergency Department,
- planning for safe use of MRIs,
- evacuating all patients from a VA medical facility, and
- reprocessing reusable medical devices.

Table 7.1. Example of Use-Related Risk Analysis

Task No.	Use Task Description	Description of Potential Use Errors	Potential Hazards/Harm and Severity	Critical Task (Yes/No)	Risk Mitigation Measure for Each Use Error	Evaluation Method in HF Validation Study
4	Press green button and hold for 10 seconds	Button is held for less than 10 seconds	Full dose is not injected; leads to patient death	Yes	Redesign product to eliminate the need to hold for 10 seconds	Evaluated in HF validation study in use scenario 1: Administration of Drug, task 4

HFMEA, designed by the VA National Center for Patient Safety specifically for health care, streamlines the hazard analysis steps found in the traditional FMEA process by combining the detectability and criticality steps into an algorithm, which is presented as a decision tree. It also replaces calculation of the risk priority number (RPN) with a hazard score that is read directly from a component the VA calls the "hazard matrix table," developed for this purpose.

So, you can see that there are many alternative terms to describe these human factors or use-related risk analysis methods.

The Role of More Detailed Analysis Using the Perception, Cognition, and Action Models

As we mentioned in Chapter 3, PCA, or analysis of human perception, cognition, and action (Card, Newell, & Moran, 1983), is a highly useful tool that you can use in conjunction with use-related risk analysis. The most important benefit is that it allows for a more granular view of the tasks analyzed in an FMEA by enabling you to divide each task into the three components that are typically involved for any human interaction with a device or system.

In addition to allowing a more nuanced description of use errors in a uFMEA or its equivalent, a PCA analysis can be valuable in helping you understand root cause analysis of use problems and ultimately guide risk mitigations that address failures in one or more categories (i.e., perception, cognition, or actions; see Reeves, Mendat, & Shaver, 2019).

PCA can be a tedious extension of a uFMEA, but some analysts feel this effort is worthwhile and can lead to much better insights into root causes of harmful use errors. Extra columns can be added to a uFMEA or any use error risk assessment immediately after the use error description column. Typically, there would be three extra columns covering the three PCA components. Harm and its severity would not be different for use errors that have different PCA root causes. This is an alternative way to incorporate PCA analysis, in contrast to the PCA example shown in Table 3.5 for an infusion pump.

Delphi Technique for Estimations

Previously, we discussed the challenges and issues involved in working with a diverse risk management team to do the difficult task of making estimates of harm severity and the even more challenging estimates of probability of occurrence of use errors.

The Delphi technique is a group forecasting methodologies generally used for future events such as technological developments. It uses estimates from experts and feedback summaries of these estimates, which allow for additional iterative estimates by these experts until reasonable consensus occurs. The following description of the Delphi technique is adapted from Israelski and Muto (2012). We suggest you can use it for achieving consensus on ratings and decisions related to risk management.

The Delphi technique was developed by the RAND Corporation in the late 1960s as a forecasting methodology. Later, the U.S. government enhanced it as a group decision-making tool with the results of Project HINDSIGHT, which established a factual basis for the workability of Delphi. That project produced a tool in which a group of experts could come to some consensus when the decisive factors were subjective and not knowledge based. The general steps in performing a Delphi technique are as follows:

1. Pick a facilitation leader.
2. Select a panel of experts.
3. Have experts independently make estimates of harm severity and harm probability of occurrence.

4. Calculate means and standard deviations.
5. Conduct a group discussion of results, focusing on differences in expert estimates.
6. Have experts repeat making independent estimates of severity and probability.
7. Recalculate means and standard deviations.
8. Reiterate process until the estimates start to show convergence or group consensus is achieved.

Other Risk Management Methods and Techniques and Their Implications

Many other methods and techniques are available for performing risk management. Here are a few of the more important ones, with some discussion about implications of their use.

HAZOPS, HACCPs, bowtie diagrams, and fishbone diagrams. Hazard and operability studies—systematic (HAZOPS) is a technique for analyzing industrial processing flows to detect deviations from design intent. This methodology uses a structured, deviation-based approach to identify possible causes and potential consequences and assign or propose appropriate mitigations to eliminate or reduce the risk associated with the respective hazard scenario. The HAZOP technique is typically documented in a tabular form using either a generic worksheet or table or commercially available HAZOP software.

Hazard analysis and critical control points, or HACCP, is used to analyze critical process control points, typically in food processing and production control. HACCP has the following steps.

- Conduct a hazard analysis.
- Identify critical control points.
- Establish critical limits.
- Establish monitoring procedures.
- Establish corrective actions.
- Establish verification procedures.
- Establish a recordkeeping procedure.

A bowtie diagram is shaped like a bowtie, creating a clear differentiation between the proactive and reactive sides of risk management. The bowtie diagram provides you with an overview of multiple plausible incident scenarios and shows which barriers (risk mitigations) you have in place to control these scenarios. See CGE Risk Management Solutions (2020) and Herber (2020) for more details.

Fishbone diagrams can also be useful in graphically showing the root causes of a hazard or a problem that you are trying to examine. These diagrams serve many purposes, including as a supplemental risk management tool. Figure 7.1 is an example of a fishbone diagram, also known as a "cause-and-effect diagram." This example displays categories of causes that can lead to the risk of infection for a person with a coronavirus such as COVID-19.

Role of preliminary hazard analysis, cognitive walkthroughs, and contextual inquiry. Among the first things a risk management team needs to do is develop a preliminary list of hazards, the related plausible hazardous situations, and the resulting harms and their severities. This hazard analysis is preceded by a thorough task analysis, as mentioned in Chapter 1 and illustrated in the AED case study in Chapter 5. Since this list is preliminary, you will need to iterate and expand it as appropriate.

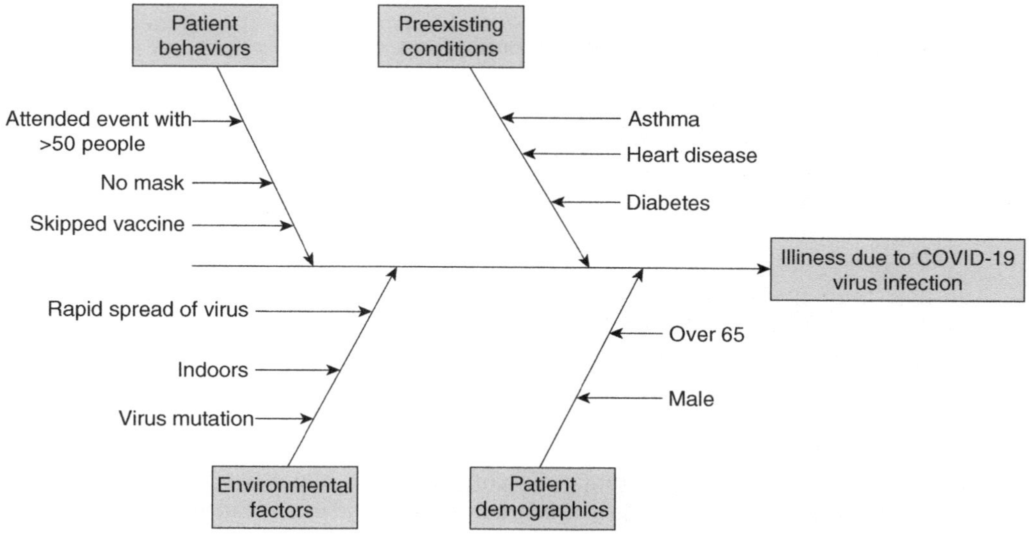

Figure 7.1. Example of a fishbone diagram of causes of risk for a coronavirus infection.

Inputs to the preliminary hazard list are known use problems with similar devices or processes that can be derived from product recalls, adverse event reports, user complaints, observed use errors in previous usability studies, and reviews of relevant literature. As we have shown in the case study, the preliminary hazard list (Table 5.3 for the AED, page 52) gets further analyzed to identify possible use-related problems, including use errors, close calls, and use difficulties.

Chapter 2 introduced the risk management process starting with the preliminary hazard analysis and progressing to the more complete analyses, including FMEAs, URRAs, and FTAs. In that chapter, we suggest lists of data sources for known use problems, including, for medical devices in the United States, the FDA's MAUDE database, which contains a record of reported severe adverse events. Similar databases in the European Union and around the world help in postmarket surveillance of these types of products. They are helpful in establishing whether or not a product recall is required and also aid in the identification of known use problems. Another very rich source of use problems comes from customer complaint files, which are typically proprietary and available only from the product manufacturer. These go beyond reports of adverse events and include a wider variety of use-related issues.

Harris and North (2012) offer useful advice on how to extract information about prior use problems from these databases, particularly MAUDE. The problem with many of these databases is that they often do not include the explicit category of "use error," and that makes finding use problems challenging. Harris and North, from their investigations of these databases, recommend using surrogate terms that can help uncover use problems. Enhancing the search for known use problems can be aided by use of the following alternative search terms (synonyms).

- Human-error-related terms, including
  - misinterpreted, unable, inability, ignore
  - failure, difficulty, corrected, error

    - forgot, training, wrong, unexpected
    - instructions, manuals, misread, misunderstood
- Task-related terms, including
    - programmed, troubleshoot, updated
    - checked, entered, re-entered
- User interface terms, including
    - display, keyboard, alarms, warnings
    - menu, touchscreen

Another human factors method—contextual inquiry—which we mentioned in Chapter 2, also can be helpful in further identifying known use problems, as well as being an excellent input to product design. During the course of contextual inquiry, in the observation and questioning of representative users performing relevant tasks in typical use environments, it is common to gain a better understanding of known use problems and their related hazards.

Finally, another well-known human factors method, cognitive walkthrough, is an excellent tool to assist in the use-related risk management process (Polson et al., 1992). It is one of the many methods for performing early formative evaluations of the user interface. We discuss more about the role of formative evaluations in analyzing risk in the next section.

Cognitive walkthroughs also have value in identifying tasks that can result in use errors that create risk. A cognitive walkthrough of the user interface starts with a task analysis, which specifies the sequence of steps or actions required by a user to accomplish a task and the system responses to those actions. The system's user interface designers and evaluators then walk through the steps as a group, asking themselves a set of questions at each step. Sometimes a few representative users may be included in the group. (Technically, when users are part of the group, it becomes a pluralistic walkthrough.)

When users are part of the evaluation group, the moderators will ask them to "think aloud" as the group steps through the tasks. (We think the description "think aloud" is more traditionally associated with the very common formative usability testing methodology.) Data are gathered during the walkthrough, and afterward, a report of potential issues is compiled. This is essentially what we do when the risk management team brainstorms about use-related risk, including estimating severity of harm and its likelihood. So, now you have another name for this methodology.

Role of formative evaluations to iterate a list of critical tasks. Formative evaluations, both analytical with expert evaluators (e.g., heuristic reviews; see Molich & Nielsen, 1990; Nielsen, 1994; and Zhang et al., 2003) and human factors expert reviews and empirical (e.g., usability) testing, are key in further developing the list of tasks that are subject to use errors. As discussed in Chapter 1, we often see that the earlier analytical methods can miss things that come to light when users try to use the prototype devices and reveal previously unanticipated user interface problems and the identification of new critical tasks and hazard-related use scenarios.

Another source of information about use risk comes from the subjective probing and comments from test participants in formative usability tests. Even when participants are successful in completing tasks with no observable use problems, subsequent probing can reveal insights into significant problems that need additional attention. This subjective probing is a way of amplifying the richness of the data gathered in formative usability tests, which are limited in sample size and therefore in opportunities to observe use problems.

In fact, the FDA recommends that product designers develop three tables before creating the URRA to estimate risk:

- Known use problems—from literature research, past experience, and database searches
- Analytical analysis—performed by skilled evaluators
- Empirical analysis—using data obtained from representative users.

In Chapter 1, the Venn diagram displayed in Figure 1.2 shows the complementary nature of combining the analytical aspects of risk analysis and empirical data collection in identifying possible use errors caused by user interface design deficiencies. The methods are synergistic and best used together to increase your chances of identifying use problems, given that each method is not perfect and can produce false-negative and false-positive identification of use errors.

Essential Tasks Versus Critical Tasks

In the medical products field, regulators in the United States and European Union emphasize the value of identifying critical tasks as an important outcome of risk analysis. These tasks, which can lead to harm if use errors are committed, must be prioritized for mitigation during design and ultimately need to be included in any validation testing. But often other tasks that are part of typical product use scenarios likewise need to be considered for possible mitigation and inclusion in usability testing. These tasks are sometimes called "essential tasks" or "noncritical tasks."

Although failed essential tasks may not lead to harm, a use scenario cannot be carried out without them. For example, it is essential to turn on the power button of a patient's vital sign monitor for it to be used successfully, even though misuse of the power button itself would not lead directly to patient harm.

Ways to Reduce a Very Large Set of Critical Tasks to a Testable Set

A challenging and interesting problem arises if you are assessing risk for a complex product for which the harm severity is high for a very long list of critical tasks. We have seen devices with more than 100 tasks during which a use error could lead to patient death, such as a catheter-based heart valve repair device and its delivery system, or a very complex large-throughput IVD blood analyzer. For some complex devices, the actual procedures can take five or more hours, and the instructions amount to more than 300 pages detailing a huge number of both essential and critical tasks.

Using the URRA approach recommended by the FDA, which prohibits use error likelihood estimates and focuses solely on harm severity, results in an enormous list of critical tasks with high harm severity. The resulting summative validation study can become impractical. The solution we have seen is to rely on the existence of multiple parallel mitigations for many of the critical tasks. These mitigations are often routine and well-practiced elements of the standard of care for minimally invasive surgeries, such as catheter-based heart valve repair systems.

One way to show the impact of the mitigations is to create fault trees as inputs to each row of tasks in the URRA or the uFMEA. You could show that high-severity outcomes can occur only when many Boolean AND gate event conditions (all events coincide at the same time) need to occur for the fault hazard to be realized. Examples might include multiple surgical team members who must check the work of other team members, or when the mandatory use of checklists for addressing the chance that a surgeon might forget important elements of critical tasks.

Some Additional Considerations for Quantitative Analysis

Why Probability of Occurrence Cannot Be Ignored in Determining Residual Risk

We have described the FDA's skepticism of manufacturer's estimates of use error probability of occurrence leading to harm. The FDA and others are greatly concerned that some manufacturers will be biased in their estimates of probability for high harm severity tasks and may tend to underestimate those probabilities. We have also acknowledged the challenge in trying to estimate the probabilities of use or human error, given the current deficiencies in our ability to accurately model and predict human behavior. The negative consequence is that some tasks with high harm severity may not be classified as critical and could be ignored for further mitigation or evaluation in summative validation testing.

That is precisely why skeptics prefer the URRA method; it eliminates probability estimates altogether and focuses exclusively on severity of harm. (We gave an example of a URRA for the glucose meter case study in Chapter 6, Table 6.2, page 83.) Describing tasks as critical based only on severity of harm makes good sense, especially from a regulator's perspective. This reasoning is understandable, but it misses an important point, and that involves trying to understand and interpret residual risk. We noted in Chapter 1 that residual risk assessment for acceptability is a crucial part of risk management. We have two choices in judging residual risk:

- Determine whether the absolute risk that remains after all practical mitigations are implemented is below our predefined level of risk acceptability, or
- judge if the relative comparison of residual risk with the product's benefits indicates that the positive benefits of the product outweigh the remaining risks.

Either way, residual risk is defined as the combination of severity of harm and the probability of use error leading to harm. That is the established definition of risk.

The notion of risk and residual risk is inextricably linked to estimates of probability. In its 2016 human factors guidance, the FDA stated:

> Use-related device hazards should be identified through preliminary analyses and evaluations. When identified, these hazards should be, to the extent possible, controlled through elimination of the hazard (designed out), **reduction in likelihood** or reduction in the severity of the resulting harm prior to initiating the human factors validation test. (FDA, 2016a, sec. 7, p. 19, emphasis added)

Furthermore,

> Human factors validation testing results indicating that serious use errors persist are not acceptable in premarket submissions unless the results are analyzed well and the submission shows that **further reduction of the errors' likelihood is not possible** or practical and that the benefits of device use outweigh the residual risks. (sec 8.1.7, p. 28, emphasis added)

As noted in Chapter 3, the vast majority of mitigations for risk involve reducing the likelihood of harm rather than reducing the severity of harm. So, it seems impossible to address the notion of acceptability of residual risk when ignoring probability of use error or, as stated in the FDA guidance, "reduction in likelihood."

If we ignore probability of harm, we are no longer evaluating residual risk. Rather, we are forced to evaluate what might be called "residual harm." This would be challenging for your risk management team and probably not practical, since reducing harm is much more difficult to accomplish. Practically, we cannot ignore probability or likelihood of use error leading to harm.

Another consideration is that many manufactures have quality control systems as part of their design control process for product design, and those systems have traditionally included formal risk management for the product design (and its design components) and for the manufacturing process itself. This risk management has traditionally taken the form of FMEAs and sometimes FTAs.

Now these same manufacturers have added use FMEA or application FMEA to their quality control systems, which requires all of the FMEA elements, including probability or likelihood of faults leading to product failure or harm. If URRAs were to be used to the exclusion of uFMEAs, those manufacturers would fail audits of their quality control systems. This is another reason that uFMEAs (with probability of occurrence ratings) need to continue to be conducted, along with URRAs extracted from them, as a way of identifying critical tasks when making submissions to the FDA.

Connection Between Use Risk Analysis and Safety Assurance Cases

Use Safety Assurance Cases

The safety assurance case is another risk management tool. According to the Association for the Advancement of Medical Instrumentation's Technical Information Report 38 (AAMI, 2014, p. ii),

> The Medical Device Safety Assurance Case outlined in this technical information report (TIR) provides a comprehensive and organized summary of product risk along with the evidence-based arguments that support the claims that the hazards that may arise from risk have either been eliminated or mitigated to the extent that the product is safe for its intended use.
>
> An assurance case includes a top-level claim for a property of a system or product (or set of claims), systematic argumentation regarding this claim, and the evidence and explicit assumptions that underlie this argumentation. Arguing through multiple levels of subordinate claims, this structured argumentation connects the top-level claim to the evidence and assumptions (ISO/IEC 15026-2:2011).
>
> An assurance case is a systematic, structured methodology for supporting a stated claim. The claim may be related to safety, reliability, maintainability, security, etc. A safety assurance case is an assurance case with a top-level claim of safety.

Some have compared the safety case to the summation that attorneys present to a jury at the conclusion of a court trial. The assurance case is usually broad and covers the complete product, but among the subclaims you will often find a claim that use-related risk has been found to be acceptable. Among the documentation methods for an assurance case is a graphical depiction or a table. AAMI TIR 38:2014 contains a generic example of a safety case in graphical format using shapes that are part of a system called "goal structuring notation."

The FDA has become a strong supporter of the use of safety assurance cases and now requires them for one class of medical devices (infusion pump systems) as part of regulatory submissions. Software packages exist that can be used in preparing these safety cases (Eagles & Wu, 2014). Safety cases are useful in analyzing high-reliability software systems that might be used in a variety of domains, including aviation and nuclear power, as well as medical devices.

Additional Areas to Apply Risk Management

As mentioned in Chapter 1, risk management is applicable to many subject domains where harm during use is possible, including aviation, space flight, nuclear power, transportation in general, health care, and consumer products. There are very well-known and much-discussed debates about the predictive ability and reliability of risk management tools. Probably the most challenging is the estimation of probability, or the likelihood of a use problem leading to harm; we and others have made the point that human behavior is complex and difficult to predict. There is also the problem of estimating system component fault probabilities by potentially conflicted members of the risk management team, as might happen when management overrides higher engineering estimates of probabilities in order to avoid delaying a mission or project.

One of the most renowned and tragic examples of this problem is the NASA *Challenger* space shuttle fatal launch from Cape Canaveral in Florida on the subfreezing morning of January 28, 1986. The likely root cause was an explosion of the solid rocket boosters in the minutes after launch due to failed O ring seals (see Feynman, 1986, and Jenab & Moslehpour, 2016, for more details). Originally, the estimates of O ring failure due to subfreezing temperatures at the launch pad were in the range from roughly 1 in 100 to 1 in 100,000. The higher probability estimates came from the working engineers, and the very low estimates came from NASA management.

Unfortunately, managers were concerned about the political implications of further launch delays and overrode the higher failure estimates in favor of the lower, more acceptable levels.

Another, more contemporary, case concerns the two Boeing 737 MAX 8 fatal air crashes in 2018–2019, in which 346 people were killed. The most likely root causes of the crashes were faulty software and pilot confusion over how to deal with the faults for an antistall automated flight control system called MCAS (maneuvering characteristics augmentation system).

The following overview is derived from a review published in the *Wall Street Journal* on December 11, 2019.

- The first fatal crash of the 737 MAX 8 was in October 2018 and involved a Lion Air flight from Jakatar, Indonesia, that killed 189 people.
- The FAA analysis predicted that over the 30–45-year lifetime of the MAX fleet globally, 15 similar accidents could occur unless fixes were made to the MCAS automated flight control system.
- The FAA analysis incorporated widely used principles, including numerical risk assessment, and considered many variables, such as pilot training and emergency reaction times and the timing of design changes to the MCAS system.
- The FAA decided to allow the MAX 8 to remain in service in anticipation of several fixes, including to the MCAS system. The agency found the risk to be sufficiently low while the retrofitting was being implemented.

- Unfortunately, a second fatal crash occurred in March 2019, in Ejere, Ethiopia, involving an Ethiopian Airlines flight in which 157 people were killed. That crash also pointed to the flawed MCAS system and the pilot's inability to control the system as the root cause.
- The FAA grounded the MAX 8 fleet. The updated risk analysis predicted two fatal accidents for every 1 million flights. The 737 model that preceded the MAX had only one crash for every 10 million flights, as reported by Boeing.

The risk analyses described in the article were based on an FAA methods handbook (FAA, 2000), which include FMEAs and FTAs. The unfortunate theme is repeated here of the challenging problem of making reliable statistically based estimates of fault probabilities.

We see this same difficult problem in other domains and cases, including the meltdown of the number 4 nuclear reactor in Chernobyl, Ukraine, in April 1986. That meltdown immediately killed at least eight people, and the radiation release eventually killed dozens more through cancers (some speculate much higher numbers, in the tens of thousands) and made the nearby town of Pryp'yat uninhabitable for many thousands of years.

The incident occurred when engineers underestimated the risks of a training experiment to see how far reactor control rods could be withdrawn before the nuclear reactor reached critical temperatures, while keeping output power at a very low level and all water-circulating cooling pumps running. It was an ill-advised experiment, done at the request of plant management for apparently political reasons, and the probability of a meltdown from an uncontrolled nuclear reaction was severely underestimated. It eventually led to substantial changes and modifications in the design of similar nuclear reactors in the former Soviet Union. Additional details may be found in Britannica (2020), Anspaugh and Goldman (1988), and U.S. Department of Energy (1987).

We can learn from the themes in these cases in order to avoid them: (a) management override of technical experts' higher fault probability estimates, usually through prioritizing schedules and budgets over safety; and (b) team dynamics influencing estimates, whereby different areas of domain knowledge may cause legitimate differences in the justification for likelihood and severity estimates.

Final Word

We hope this book has accomplished the objective of serving as a user guide for understanding the goals and principles of risk management, including risk analysis, evaluation, and control. Through detailed implementation instructions and representative case studies, we have detailed how you can implement the most common risk management tools, including use-related FMEAs, URRAs, and FTAs.

As we have described throughout this book, the rigorous application of the methods—with strict adherence to the principles outlined here—should guide your use of these important risk assessment methods. You should take care to avoid mixing political or business considerations as you do this work to help ensure that the output of these assessments is as accurate and informative as possible.

Recommended Readings

Works in bold type are highly recommended.

Andre, A. D., Jorgenson, D. B., Froman, J. A., Snyder, D. E., & Poole, J. E. (2004). Automated external defibrillator use by untrained bystanders: Can the public-use model work? *Prehospital Emergency Care*, *8*(3), 284–291.

Association for the Advancement of Medical Instrumentation. (2010). *Human factors engineering: Design of medical devices* (ANSI/AAMI HE75:2009). AAMI.

Bailey, R. W. (1983). *Human error in computer systems*. Prentice Hall.

Casey, S. M. (1998). *Set phasers on stun: And other true tales of design, technology, and human error*. Aegean.

Clemen, R. T. (1997). *Making hard decisions: An introduction to decision analysis*. Duxbury.

Cox, L. A., Jr., Babayev, D., & Huber, W. (2005). Some limitations of qualitative risk rating systems. *Risk Analysis*, *25*(3): 651–662.

Gardner-Bonneau, D., Weinger, M. B., & Wiklund, M. E. (Eds.). (2010). *Handbook of human factors in medical device design*. CRC Press.

International Electroctechnical Commission. (IEC). (2003). *Medical electrical equipment—Part 1–8: General requirements for safety: Alarm systems—requirements, tests and guidelines—General requirements and guidelines for alarm systems in medical electrical equipment and in medical electrical systems* (IEC 60601-1-8). IEC.

International Electrotechnical Commission. (IEC). (2016). *Medical devices—Part 2: Guidance on the application of usability engineering to medical devices* (IEC TR 62366-2). IEC.

Israelski, E. W. (2010). Testing and evaluation. In D. Gardner-Bonneau, M. B. Weinger, & M. E. Wiklund (Eds.), *Handbook of human factors in medical device design*. CRC Press

Israelski, E. W., & Muto, W. H. (2003). Use-error focused risk analysis for medical devices: A case study of the Therac-25 radiation therapy system. In *Proceedings of the Human Factors and Ergonomics Society 47th Annual Meeting* (pp. 1564–1568). Human Factors and Ergonomics Society.

Israelski, E. W., & Muto, W. H. (2011). Human factors engineering: A case study. In T. Pawlicki et al. (Eds.), *Quality and safety in radiology* (pp. 235–240). Taylor & Francis.

Leveson, N. (1995). *Safeware: System safety and computers*. Addison-Wesley.

McDermott, R. E., Mikulak, R. J., & Beauregard, M. R. (1996). *The basics of FMEA*. Productivity, Inc.

Miller, D. P., & Swain, A. D. (1987). Human error and human reliability. In G. Salvendy (Ed.), *Handbook of human factors*. Wiley.

Privitera, M. B. (Ed.). (2019). *Applied human factors in medical device design*. Elsevier.

U.S. Food and Drug Administration. (2004). *Code of Federal Regulations, 21 CFR 820, Title 21, Vol. 8. Quality system regulations, medical devices*. U.S. Department of Health and Human Services.

Wiklund, M. E., Birmingham, L., & Larsen, S. A. (2018). *Writing human factors plans & reports for medical technology development*. Association for the Advancement of Medical Instrumentation.

Wiklund, M. E., Dwyer, A., & Davis, E. (2016). *Medical device use error: Root cause analysis*. CRC Press.

Wiklund, M. E., Kendler, J., & Strochlic, A. Y. (2010). *Usability testing of medical devices*. CRC Press.

Wiklund, M. E., & Wilcox, S. B. (2000). *Designing usability into medical products*. Taylor & Francis.

References

AED Superstore. (2017). *The ultimate AED buyers guide.* https://www.aedsuperstore.com/resources/aed-buyers-guide/

American Heart Association. (2013). *Every second counts: Rural and community access to emergency devices* (AHA/HPFS/3/2013). https://nanopdf.com/download/facts-every-second-counts-rural-and-community-access-to_pdf

Anspaugh, C., & Goldman, M. (1988). The global impact of the Chernobyl reactor accident. *Science, 242*(4885): 1513–1519.

Association for the Advancement of Medical Instrumentation. (AAMI). (2014). *Medical device safety assurance case report guidance* (AAMI TIR 38). AAMI.

Britannica Editors. (2020). Chernobyl disaster nuclear accident, Soviet Union 1986. https://www.britannica.com/event/Chernobyl-disaster

Card, S. K., Newell, A., & Moran, T. P. (1983). *The psychology of human-computer interaction.* Erlbaum.

CGE Risk Management Solutions. (2020). *BowTieXP software.* https://www.wolterskluwer.com/en/solutions/enablon/bowtie

DeRosier J., et al. (2002, May). Using health care failure mode and effect analysis: The VA National Center for Patient Safety's prospective risk analysis system. *Joint Commission Journal on Quality Improvement, 28*: 248–267.

Eagles, S., & Wu, F. (2014, January). *Safety assurance cases for medical devices. Biomedical instrumentation and technology.* AAMI.

Edwards, E. T., Edwards, E. S., Davis, E., Mulcare, M., Wiklund, M., and Kelley, G. (2015). Comparative usability study of a novel auto-injector and an intranasal system for naloxone delivery. *Pain and Therapy, 4*(1): 89–105.

Feynman, R. P. (1986). *Report of the Presidential Commission on the space shuttle* Challenger *accident, vol. 2: Appendix F—Personal observations on reliability of shuttle.* U.S. Government Printing Office. https://ntrs.nasa.gov/citations/19860015255

Goldman, M., Catlin, R. J., & Anspaugh, L. (1987). *Health and environmental consequences of the Chernobyl nuclear power plant accident* (Report No. DOE/ER-0332). U.S. Department of Energy Office of Health and Environmental Research. https://www.osti.gov/biblio/6329192

Harris, S. D., & North, R. A. (2012). Mining MAUDE: Human factors perspectives on HER and device design from the FDA Manufacturers and Users Device Experience database. In *Proceedings of the 2012 Symposium on Human Factors and Ergonomics in Health Care* (pp. 1–7). Human Factors and Ergonomics Society.

Heber, P. (2020) *Bow tie diagram shapes stencil and template.* https://www.paulherber.co.uk/visio-bowtie/example.php

Hoke, R., Heinroth, K., Trappe, H., & Werdan, K. (2009). Is external defibrillation an electric threat for bystanders? *Resuscitation, 80*(4): 395–401.

International Electrotechnical Commission. (IEC). (2015). *Medical devices—Part 1: Application of usability engineering to medical devices* (IEC 62366-1). IEC.

International Organization for Standardization. (ISO). (2011). *Systems and software engineering—Systems and software assurance—Part 2: Assurance case* (ISO/IEC 15026-2:2011). ISO.

International Organization for Standardization. (ISO). (2019). *Medical devices—Application of risk management to medical devices* (ISO 14971:2019). ISO.

Israelski, E. W., & Muto, W. H. (2012). Human factors risk management in medical devices. In P. Carayon (Ed.), *Handbook of human factors and ergonomics in healthcare and patient safety* (2nd ed.). Erlbaum.

Jenab, K., & Moslehpour, S. (2016). Failure analysis: Case study *Challenger* SRB field joint. *International Journal of Engineering and Technology, 8*(6): 401–405.

Kirwan, B., & Ainsworth, L. K. (Eds.). (1992). *A guide to task analysis*. Taylor & Francis.

Kortum, P. (2016). *Usability assessment: How to measure the usability of products, services, and systems*. Human Factors and Ergonomics Society.

Makary, M. A., & Daniel, M. (2016). Medical error—The third leading cause of death in the US (analysis). *British Medical Journal, 353*: i2139. https://www.bmj.com/content/353/bmj.i2139

Molich, R., & Nielsen, J. (1990). Improving a human-computer dialogue. *Communications of the ACM, 33*(3): 338–348.

National Aeronautics and Space Administration. (NASA). (1986). *Report to the president: Actions to implement the recommendations of the Presidential Commission on the Space Shuttle* Challenger *Accident*. NASA.

National Aeronautics and Space Administration. (NASA). (2002). *Fault tree handbook with aerospace applications*. NASA Office of Safety and Mission Assurance.

Nielsen, J. (1994). Enhancing the explanatory power of usability heuristics. In *CHI '94: Proceedings of the SIGCHI Conference on Human Factors in Computing Systems* (pp. 152–158). Association for Computing Machinery. https://doi.org/10.1145/191666.191729

Pasztor, A., & Tangel, A. (2019, December 11). Internal FAA review saw high risk of 737 MAX crashes. *Wall Street Journal*.

Phillips-Medisize, LLC, & U|Sensus, LLC. (2018, March). *Anatomy of a good use error risk assessment*. http://cms.hfes.org/Cms/media/CmsImages/Anatomy-of-A-Good-Use-Error-Risk-Assessment_Phillips-Medisize-Usensus.pdf

Polson, P. G., Lewis, C., Rieman, J., & Wharton, C. (1992). Cognitive walkthroughs: A method for theory-based evaluation of user interfaces. *International Journal of Man-Machine Studies, 36*(5): 741–773.

Reason, J. T. (2013). *A life in error: From little slips to big disasters*. Ashgate.

Reeves, T., Mendat, C., & Shaver, E. (2019). Root cause analysis. In M. B. Privitera (Ed.), *Applied human factors in medical device design* (pp. 219–236). Elsevier.

Sanders, M. S., & McCormick, E. J. (1993). *Human factors in engineering and design* (7th ed.). McGraw-Hill.

Schmidt, M. W. (2004). The use and misuse of FMEA in risk analysis. *Medical Device and Diagnostics Industry, 26*(3). https://www.mddionline.com/testing/use-and-misuse-fmea-risk-analysis

Shore, W. H. (1994). *Mysteries of life and the universe: New essays from America's finest writers on science*. Harcourt Brace.

Stamatis, D. H.(1995). *Failure mode and effect analysis: FMEA from theory to execution*. ASQ Quality Press.

Stuster, J. (2019). *Task analysis: How to develop an understanding of work*. Human Factors and Ergonomics Society.

U.S. Federal Aviation Administration. (FAA). (2000, December 30). Analysis techniques. In *System safety handbook* (chap. 9). FAA.

U.S. Food and Drug Administration. (FDA). (2012). *Factors to consider when making benefit-risk determinations in medical device premarket approval and de novo classifications*. FDA.

U.S. Food and Drug Administration. (FDA). (2016a). *Applying human factors and usability engineering to medical devices*. FDA.

U.S. Food and Drug Administration. (FDA). (2016b). *Factors to consider regarding benefit-risk in medical device product availability, compliance, and enforcement decisions* (draft). FDA.

U.S. Food and Drug Administration. (FDA). (2018). *Contents of a complete submission for threshold analyses and human factors submissions to drug and biologic applications* (draft). FDA.

U.S. Food and Drug Administration. (FDA). (2020a). MAUDE—Manufacturer and user facility. https://www.accessdata.fda.gov/scripts/cdrh/cfdocs/cfmaude/search.cfm

U. S. Nuclear Regulatory Commission. (NRC). (1981). *Fault tree handbook*. NRC.

Wickens, C., Lee, J., Liu, Y. D., & Gordon-Becker, S. (2004). *Introduction to human factors engineering* (2nd ed.) Pearson Education.

Zhang, J., et al. (2003). Using usability heuristics to evaluate patient safety of medical devices. *Journal of Biomedical Informatics*, *36*: 23–30.

Index

About the Authors

Edmond W. Israelski is the retired director of human factors at the biopharmaceutical firm AbbVie, where he led a cross-company team to embed best-practice human factors engineering design methods into all of the firm's products to ensure safety and usability. AbbVie's Volwiler Society awarded him a Lifetime Achievement Award in 2016. In his current role as a consultant, Israelski provides strategic advice to medical product developers to ensure compliance with international standards and regulatory requirements of the U.S. Food and Drug Administration. He is the co-convener for the International Electrochemical Commission and International Standards Organization ergonomics and usability engineering groups in the development of international human factors/usability medical devices standards. Ed is also past cochair of the Association for the Advancement of Medical Instrumentation Human Factors Engineering Committee, which develops human factors standards for medical devices. A Certified Human Factors Professional, Ed holds 30 patents, is a fellow of the Human Factors and Ergonomics Society, and is a past member of the National Academy of Sciences Board on Human-Systems Integration. He is on the editorial board of the journal *Human Factors* and serves as a regular reviewer for several other scientific journals. He received a BS in electrical engineering from NJIT, an MS in operations research from Columbia University, and a PhD in industrial and engineering psychology from Stevens Institute of Technology.

William H. Muto retired after 22 years as a principal human factors engineer at Abbott Laboratories, a manufacturer of a medical devices and products. During his tenure at Abbott, while playing a key role in the design and evaluation of a wide variety of medical products, he helped to establish human factors as a core discipline in the company and assisted in the development of corporate-wide human factors policies and procedures. Prior to Abbott, Bill held management and senior engineering positions at Texas Instruments and Xerox Corporation. He holds a PhD in industrial engineering (with a human factors specialty) from Virginia Tech. He is a Certified Professional Ergonomist and fellow of the Human Factors and Ergonomics Society. Muto served for more than 15 years on the Association for the Advancement of Medical Instrumentation Human Factors Engineering Committee and is a past director and officer of the Board of Certification in Professional Ergonomics.

Made in the USA
Las Vegas, NV
10 November 2026

57843100R00066